Managing Public-Private Partnerships

This concise textbook provides a comprehensive framework for understanding and implementing effective public-private partnerships in an era of complex policy challenges and resource constraints. Drawing on research and empirical evidence, it examines how cross-sector collaboration has evolved from traditional contracting relationships to strategic partnerships that create substantial public value.

This book offers a systematic typology of partnership models, analytical tools for partnership evaluation, and practical strategies for collaborative leadership. It integrates theoretical foundations with actionable insights on partnership formation, governance structures, and performance management across diverse policy domains including healthcare, cities, and climate initiatives. Each chapter includes suggested reading and discussion questions.

Designed primarily for graduate and advanced undergraduate students in public administration, public policy, and business management programmes, this volume also serves as an essential resource for public managers and policy practitioners.

Carsten Greve is a Professor of Public Management and Governance at Copenhagen Business School, Denmark.

Masters in Public Management

Series Editor: Stephen P. Osborne

Providing students and practitioners a series of concise and coordinated learning resources, this series offers an integrated and up-to-date collection of applied textbooks across public management and administration.

Books in the series go beyond the "toolkit" or "recipe" format, instead encouraging readers to develop the core managerial skills and critical thinking required to excel in the field.

Strategic Management in the Public Sector
Paul Joyce

Performance Management in the Public Sector, Third Edition
Wouter Van Dooren, Geert Bouckaert and John Halligan

Strategic Leadership in the Public Sector
Paul Joyce

Marketing Management and Communications in the Public Sector
Martial Pasquier and Jean-Patrick

Digital Government
Managing Public Sector Reform in the Digital Era
Miriam Lips

Research Methods in Public Administration and Public Management
An Introduction
Sandra van Thiel

Financial Management and Accounting in the Public Sector, Third Edition
Gary Bandy

Risk and Crisis Management in the Public Sector, Third Edition
Lynn T. Drennan, Adina Dudau, Allan McConnell and Alistair Stark

Managing Public-Private Partnerships
Carsten Greve

For more information about this series, please visit: www.routledge.com/Routledge-Masters-in-Public-Management/book-series/PUBMAN

Managing Public-Private Partnerships

Carsten Greve

Routledge
Taylor & Francis Group
LONDON AND NEW YORK

First published 2026
by Routledge
4 Park Square, Milton Park, Abingdon, Oxon OX14 4RN

and by Routledge
605 Third Avenue, New York, NY 10158

Routledge is an imprint of the Taylor & Francis Group, an informa business

British Library Cataloguing-in-Publication Data
A catalogue record for this book is available from the British Library

ISBN: 978-0-367-89749-9 (hbk)
ISBN: 978-0-367-89750-5 (pbk)
ISBN: 978-1-003-02084-4 (ebk)

DOI: 10.4324/9781003020844

Typeset in Times New Roman
by codeMantra

Contents

1 Partnering for public action

Global challenges, managerial responses

Learning objectives

By the end of this chapter you should:

- Have an understanding of how partnerships are defined
- Be clearer about the reasons of why organizations want or need to partner up
- Get a sense of the variety of partnerships that is out there
- Have a sense of the concepts of wicked problems and the policy state which form the context that partnerships exist in

Key points of this chapter

- Partnership definitions come in many shapes and sizes, but they all circle around some of the same elements that involve responding to a complex world, collaborating, and focusing on some sort of public value.
- A typology of five different types of partnerships suggests a useful avenue for understanding the variety of partnerships.
- Both wicked problems and the advent of the policy state are conditions that influence why partnerships are necessary in today's complex world.

DOI: 10.4324/9781003020844-1

Key terms

- A useful starting point in definitions is one that sees partnerships as "the linking and sharing of information, resources, activities, and capabilities by organizations in two or more sectors to achieve jointly at outcome that could not be achieved by organizations in one sector separately", according to John Bryson et al. (2006: 44)
- Partnerships come in the form of infrastructure public-private partnerships (IPPP), public-private policy partnerships (PPPP), public-private innovation partnerships (PPIP), public-private service partnerships (PPSP), and development public-private partnerships (DPPP).
- Wicked problems are complex, intractable, open-ended, unpredictable (Alford & Head 2017: 398). The concept of the policy state introduces the need for governments to collaborate with many types of organizations because governments want to get stuff done and cannot do it all by themselves.

Introduction

This chapter focuses on why partnerships have become so crucial for public managers to engage in. Partnerships are not only initiated for economic and resource reasons but also for strategic reasons that align public managers with their key stakeholders. The chapter also references the current discussion of linking public sector organizations to the wider UN Sustainable Development Goals which have "Partnerships for all the goals" as Goal #17. The chapter outlines a process-based model on partnerships, based on the available sources in the literature on partnerships.

A seminal definition came from Dutch scholars, Klijn and Teisman, who said that PPPs were "more or less sustainable co-operation between public and private actors in which joint products and/or services are developed and in which risks, costs and profits are shared" (Klijn and Teisman 2003: 137, cited from Klijn 2022: 33). Klijn also distinguished between PPPs as a monitoring game, as collaboration and as sense-making.

Public-private partnerships have been defined as organizations that work together for a common goal. A widely used definition comes from Bryson et al. that emphasizes the collaboration part: "the linking and sharing of information, resources, activities, and capabilities by organizations in two or more sectors to achieve jointly at outcome that could not be achieved by organizations in one sector separately" (Bryson, Crosby and Bloomberg 2015: 648, based on Crosby et al. 2006: 44).

Another definition comes from the *Journal of Management* which emphasizes the hybrid nature of the relationship. "Interorganizational arrangements pursuing social and economic objectives through various forms of formal or informal relationships between public-, for-profit and non-profit firms" (Quelin, Kivleniece and Lazzarine 2017: 767).

A related definition is: "Relatively intensive, long-term interactions between organizations from at least two sectors (business, government and/or civil society) aimed at addressing a social or environmental problem" (Clarke and Crane 2018: 303).

In her recent book on *Collaboration and Public Policy*, Helen Sullivan (2022) discusses collaboration and partnerships at length, and has the following definitions.

Collaboration has been defined as "the coming together of actors to work across boundaries in pursuit of public purpose" (Sullivan and Skelcher 2002, 2). A more elaborated definition is offered by Sullivan as well: "more-or-less stable configurations of rules, resources and relationships generated, negotiated and reproduced by diverse, yet interdependent actors that enables them to act together in the pursuit of public purposes" (Sullivan 2022, Chapter 1).

As Sullivan also writes: "The agency is not unfettered, actors operate within and between existing structures of power, so their agency is always situated (Sullivan et al. 2012), but it acts on structural power and can influence it" (Sullivan 2022, Chapter 1).

An early definition by the Organisation for Economic Co-operation and Development (OECD) from 1990 (cited in McQuaid 2009:128) is:

> Systems of formalised co-operation, grounded in legally binding arrangements or informal understandings, co-operative working relationship and mutually adopted plans among a number of institutions. They involve agreements on policy and programme objectives and the sharing of responsibility, resources, risks and benefits over a specified period of time.

If this definition has used "rewards" instead of "benefits", it may have been called the sharing of the 4Rs.

The literature in the area of PPPs, collaboration, and networks is wide. All sub-literatures have a lot in common, but they also differ in a number of ways. Partnerships studies tend to focus on how partners get together for mostly pragmatic reasons to solve problems. Collaboration studies are more concerned with the nature of the collaboration itself and what factors facilitate the collaboration. Network studies tend to be more attentive to the structural side of networks and how many actors are in a network – and which ones are outside the network. Page and Stone (2023) have recently suggested the term "collaborative architecture" as an overarching term for the different varieties of literatures.

Most of the literature suggests that PPPs work towards producing public value. The public value is mostly associated with the works of Harvard professor Mark Moore (1995, 2013). The Bryson, Crosby, and Bloomberg's (2015) synthesis also incorporates the concept of public value. There is often a fine distinction between public value and public values in the plural where the latter comes from the literature represented by Bozeman (2007). In a recent contribution, Brewer (2025) suggested that they can be combined. There are now many works on what public value means and how it can be interpreted (see, for example, Sancino 2022; Greve and Ysa 2023).

For various reasons these literatures on PPPs have developed side by side. There are some great overviews of the debates in many publications, including from Klijn and Koppenjan and from Nabogh and Nabatchi. There are also some great attempts at making synthesizers. These come mainly from Bryson et al. and from the *Journal of Management* that vows to make more coherent models and unite different approaches.

For the purpose of this book, which emphasizes the pragmatic approach to partnerships that create public value, we stick to the Bryson definition mentioned above that have been developed in several publications.

Why do organizations need to partner up?

There are several reasons why organizations need to work together. Forrer, Kee, and Boyer (2015) list three main reasons; Pragmatic, strategic and economical. The first one is the pragmatic reason: organizations work together in partnerships because it makes sense as they cannot solve a problem on their own. Organizations need other organizations and so they work together. This is also the premise of this book. Partnership arrives when there is a pragmatic need to do it. The second reason can be that organizations think strategically and want to become partners with other organizations that might benefit their overall strategy. This way, organizations can set their mind to work on a specific project in which they need a specific partner or group of partners to succeed. The third reason can be that it serves an economic purpose: It can simply be more cost efficient to partner up and collaborate. Williamsons' well-known transaction cost theory is relevant here. Tasks need to be taken care of where there are least transaction costs. That could be through markets or through hierarchies, but it could also be in hybrid organizational forms such as partnerships.

McQuaid (2009: 138–142) listed a number of key success factors for partnerships: a clear strategic focus; strategic leadership and support; the importance of trust, organizations and people in partnerships; capacity for co-operation and mutualism; organizational complementarity; incentives for partners and "symbiotic interdependency"; the value of action and the outcome-oriented procedures.

In countries where the public governance paradigms have been influenced by New Public Management and a greater gulf has been created between the public sector and the private sector, there may be a more urgent need to try to collaborate and partner up again. This can be contrasted to countries, like the Scandinavian countries, where there is much experience with collaborations and where partnerships between the public sector and the private sector almost come natural.

The reasons why organizations enter into partnerships must be analysed in the context that they are in. There is no strict causal relationship between an organization's place in society and its inclination to partner up with other organizations.

Using a broad collaboration approach, Kekez, Howlett, and Ramesh (2018: table 2) identify six ways to collaborate: consultative in-house delivery, contracting out, commissioning, co-management, co-production, third party certification. They identify three levels of policy and governance capacity: analytical competencies, managerial competencies, and political competencies. At the individual managerial level, the competencies are: motivation and ability of service providers to engage in creation of knowledge and quality in partnership with citizens and civil society.

Beth Simone Noveck (2021: 261–271) points to the following reasons for making a partnership: cost savings, improved service delivery, better expertise, working differently, more hands on deck, sharing data, and access to tech.

The policy state

American researchers Orren and Skowronek (2017) have come up with the term "the policy state" to explain why politicians make so much policy. For politicians, it is of course natural to make policy. That's what they are there for. But Orren and Skowronek point out that politicians nowadays have few things that hold them back. If politicians come across an obstacle, they want to circumvent it, even if it is an existing law. Politicians, in former president Obama's words, want "to get stuff done". And there is so much demand on action from citizens who want to see problems solved.

> The priority of policy is for them just common sense: the nation faces serious problems on every front. It is the responsibility of government to respond and where necessary adapt; refusing to engage in the constructive search for solutions is not a serious option.
>
> (Orren and Skowronek 2017: 4)

Politicians and governments face so many challenges today, and the expectation from companies and citizens is that politicians step up and come forward with solutions that can address those challenges. Orren and Skowronek remark that the policy state has increased in activity: "Put simply, we argue that policy has expanded its role in American government and society by eroding the boundaries and dissolving the distinctions that once constrained policy's reach" (Orren and Skowronek 2017: 6).

The definition of policy is: "Policy is a commitment to a designated goal or course of action made authoritatively on behalf of a given entity or collectivity and accompanied by guidelines for its accomplishments" (Orren and Skowronek 2017: 27).

Orren and Skowronek (2017: 28) point out that "policy is animated by discontent with the status quo, by circumstances as they unfold, by problems as they arise". Governments respond to challenges in the order that they meet them and try to intervene or suggest action to remedy the problems. As they say a little later: "The policy motive is open-ended, instrumental, calculating and creative; it seeks efficiency and anticipates more policy to come" (Orren and Skowronek 2017: 28).

There are some restrictions towards policy traditionally. One obstacle is "rights": Orren and Skowronek define them the following way:

> Rights are claims that one person, in or outside government, may make on the person or actions of another, enforceable in a court of law (Orren and Skowronek 2017: 29). Another is "structure", defined as "an entire ensemble, a comprehensive scheme or interrelated pieces with its own discernable "principles" of organization.
>
> (Orren and Skowronek 2017: 33)

What has the policy state to do with partnerships? A lot it turns out. The policy state is also an enduring reforming state: reorganization and new initiatives are essential because policy solutions are put forward by politicians on a continuing basis. Policy therefore weakens both rights and structure according to Orren. There will be constant changes because new policies will be formulated and enacted. Reform – or what they refer to as rearrangement is always on the agenda:

> Rearrangement is policy's beat, promoting an inveterate hostility to fixed relationships of any kind.
>
> (Orren and Skowronek 2017: 35)

Because politicians are active proposing and finding solutions to challenges, they often see existing legislation as a hindrance. Orren and Skowronek use a gambling metaphor when they explain that rights are not trumps anymore, but bargaining chips. A trump is something that clears the table and says – here to and no further. But a chip can be used in a bargaining game.

The constant reform or rearrangement impulse is what drives governments nowadays. And because governments' own structures or set of organizations cannot handle all the tasks that governments have promised with their new policies, governments need to rely on PPPs instead. PPPs are here seen as prolonging of the state. They are shock absorbers in a way, because governments have to rely private sector partners to "get the stuff done" on the ground that governments have decided upon. This could very well be the primary reasons why we observe the continuous development of new PPPs. Partnerships are there for a reason: To help governments fulfil their promises. A tag line could be "more policy, more partnerships". Policies breed new partnerships.

Orren and Skowronek (2017: 106) contend themselves that "administration is the outgrowth of policy, and administrative agencies extend policy making beyond the government's three-branch structure". Here, we argue that extension of administration in practice mean PPPs. In their many forms, PPPs can help governing promises made in the policy state.

The idea of extension of government by other means dates back, at least to Frederick C. Mosher's article in *Public Administration Review* which argued that the US federal government was carrying out its tasks through "non-federal institutions and individuals" in what they term "catalytic government" (Eggers and Kettl 2023: Chapter 5).

Wicked problems

The advent of wicked problems also creates incentives to partnerships. A great point of reference in public management and governance has centred on the issue of wicked problems and how the presence of wicked problems has incentivized organizations to partner up. The concept of wicked problems dates back to the 1970s to Rittel and Webber's approach (Alford and Head 2017; Winther 2025). They saw that many problems were not immediately solvable and that single organizations were struggling with coming to terms with how to handle wicked problems. The notion of wicked problems has been underlined by the events of recent years with the pandemic and what Alasdair Roberts (2020) refer to as "the third and fatal shock" to what he calls "the millennial paradigm". The millennial paradigm translates into the neo-liberal era that was dominated by the Washington consensus. Globalization and spread of markets were all the rage. Less state interference and less regulation was the order of the day. But several crises hit, and now the crises have come so fast that Alasdair Roberts now talks of the end of the millennial paradigm. The crises mentioned by Alasdair Roberts include the terror attacks on 9/11 and beyond, the global financial crisis in 2008–2009, and now the corona crisis with the global paradigm. In Alasdair Roberts' understanding, these are not just fleeing crisis that will be overcome after which we all go back to normal. The turbulence is the new normal and with the climate crisis as perhaps the biggest and longest crisis of them all, there is no chance that things will settle down again and just get back to where it was before.

All of this points to the relevance of discussing wicked problems: problems that cannot easily be tamed, and that often require collaboration and partnerships to be addressed. In the public management and governance literature, the approach by Head and Alford has won great recognition. In a table, they differ between the degree of the problem itself and the number of actors that are needed. This gives them a possibility to distinguish between less wicked problems, wicked problems, and super wicked problems. The Alford and Head's table approach provides a good starting point for us here. You can examine what type of problem your own organization is facing and how many other organizations you need to collaborate with to address the issue.

What partnerships can do to address wicked problems?

So now you get the picture. There are wicked problems out there that no single organization can solve. There is therefore an incentive for organizations to work more closely together. Organizations do this when they form partnerships. The reasons for forming partnerships are mostly pragmatic, but they can be both economic and strategic. We now need a more elaborate model to work from, as shown in the following chapters. The inspiration for this model comes from Bryson et al. who distinguishes between the basic foundations for a partnership, the management and process of a partnership, the structure and governance of a partnership, the context and limitations for a partnership, and the public value created in the end out of a partnership.

The foundations include the institutional context and the need to address wicked problems. The management and the processes include identifying together what the challenge consists of and finding a shared understanding of the problem. It also consists of creating legitimacy for one's actions as a key managerial task. Managerial tasks also include to find a common narrative that the partnership can adhere to and to build the organizational capacity or operational capacity to make sure that the partnership's tasks can be carried out. It also means dealing with other parties or organizations that are against the ideas that the partnership is trying to promote. Next is the governance structure which includes the structure of the partnership itself. A solid governance structure will often include some sort of board or advisory committee where the key stakeholders can meet and debate the direction of the partnership. Finally, there is the implementation of the partnership's strategy and the identification of the public value that the partnership creates. The public value needs to be recognized by a third party often, but the different partners also must share an understanding of what the different partners can get out of the partnership themselves.

A typology of partnerships

We have been talking about the partnerships that solve or at least address wicked problems. But what about the many types of partnerships that we know that exist? Throughout the years researchers have been grappling with and documenting a variety of partnership forms. Brinkerhoff and Brinkerhoff (2011) came up with a typology that seems useful and covers most of the variants that we see: (1) policy partnerships, (2) service partnerships, (3) infrastructure partnerships, (4) urban development partnerships, and (5) development partnerships.

In this book, we will distinguish between the following types of partnerships here:

- **Infrastructure** public-private partnerships (IPPP)
- Public-private **policy** partnerships (PPPP)
- Public-private **innovation** partnerships (PPIP)
- Public-private **service** partnerships (PPSP)
- **Development** public-private partnerships (DPPP)

Infrastructure partnerships are perhaps the most talked about, and most researched of the partnership types. Here, often large, infrastructure projects are designed, built, financed, operated, and maintained in a close partnership between the public sector and the private sector (Hodge and Greve 2019, 2022). A special company is often formed – a "special purpose vehicle" in the jargon of the PPP literature – and risks are shared and value for money is the key objective.

Policy partnership is a type of partnership that addresses policy issues and wicked public policy problems.

> Public-private policy partnerships have in common a shared responsibility for policy that impacts citizens. Authentic partnering, in theory, involves close collaboration and the combination of both the private sector (more competitive and efficient) and the public sector (responsibility and accountability vis-à-vis society.
>
> (Vaillaincourt Rosenau 1999: 12)

Service partnerships have much to do with contracting for public services. Private sector companies or non-governmental organizations (NGOs) provide a service to the public based on a specific contract with the government. If this contract is more relational, then it can be called a service partnership. In this book, we argue that many type of service contracting today implies relationships between the parties to the contract, and also that many contracts for public services delivery require careful consideration, negotiation, and monitoring. Governments have to be "smart buyers" in the words of Donald Kettl (1993), and this implies a different relationship that just between a buyer and a provider. Contracts are increasingly complex and relational. Brown, Potoski, and Van Slyke name the more strict approach as "the rule camp" and the collaborative approach as "the relationship camp" and characterize the latter in the following way:

> For the relationship camp, a contract is at its core a relationship in which a buyer and a seller must each behave in the spirit of cooperation to achieve the promise of win-win gains. Win-win outcomes occur because buyers and sellers purse value for long-term mutual gain, even if sometimes at their own short-term expense, confident that in the long run their good behaviour will be rewarded in the current contract or by building a reputation for providing value that will win future contracts.
>
> (Brown, Potoski and Van Slyke 2013: 8)

Innovation partnerships are used for developing city areas and have a long history as being partnerships (Brogaard 2017). Innovation partnerships have been defined the following way: "public-private collaborations in which government and business constitute mutual partners based on complementary skills and resources" (Brogaard 2021: 135 cited in Alonso and Andrews 2022). There are three focus points in Alonso and Andrews' research: PPIPs have become an important tool for governments for innovation purposes. PPIPs require careful management. PPIPs require strong contract and performance management capabilities.

The full definition from Brogaard (2021: 135) reads as this:

> Several characteristics distinguish PPIs from other forms of public-private interaction: Most importantly, government and business constitute mutual development partners based on complementary skills and resources with innovation as the main goal (…). This entails that the public partner becomes a testbed for new solutions and provides inputs from citizens and professionals, whereas the business represents the technical knowhow and innovation skills (…).

The recent focus on smart cities, which we will return to in a later chapter, can be seen as a continuation of this trend.

Development partnerships focus on the many different ways that PPPs are being introduced in the developing world, often encouraged or suggested by organizations like the World Bank. Development PPPs can be defined the following way: "More or less formalized collaborations between government, business and/or third sector organizations based on shared knowledge, competencies and risks, and developed with the purpose of accomplishing long-term social and/or economic development in developing countries" (Brogaard and Petersen 2018) (Table 1.1).

Table 1.1 Management challenges in the different forms of partnerships

Type of partnership	*Characteristic*	*Management challenge*
IPPP	Institutional complexity in large/ mega infrastructure projects	Managing institutional complexity, risks and finances
PPPP	Policy state and wicked policy problems	Managing processes for making new policy solutions for citizens
PPIP	Fostering innovation	Managing and building innovation opportunities
PPSP	Delivering stellar public service	Managing complex contracts
DPPP	Helping developing countries	Managing the fight against corruption and promoting good governance

The new kids on the block

New ways to collaborate in partnerships have emerged in recent years. They fit with the partnership definitions presented in this chapter, but their form and purpose offer slightly different takes on what a partnership is. But they are not necessarily called partnerships as such. Among the newcomers are:

- Social Impact Bonds (SIBs) – links to IPPPs, PPIPs, and PPSPs
- Hybrids – links to PPPPs, PPIPs, and PPSPs
- Ecosystems – links to PPPPs and PPSPs

Social impact bonds (SIBs) have been described the following way: "Social Impact Bonds (SIBs) are an innovation wherein in theory private investment instead of governing funding is leveraged to fund social interventions" (Wilson et al. 2020: 179). They continue: "SIBs are partially meant to offer a substitution for existing or an alternative form of resources for commissioners and providers looking to deliver their public services" (Wilson et al. 2020: 180). SIBs do not seem to have spread as wide as maybe the buzz surrounding SIBs have indicated. According to Wilson et al. (2020: 181):

> One conclusion that can be drawn from this carefully cultivated collection (special issue in Public Money and Management 2020, ed.) is that SIBs remain (and may in reality always be) a relatively small part of the wider mix of conversations surrounding social policy, social investment and social impact.

Sinclair et al. are critical of what they see as "unwarranted enthusiasm for SIBs", and they conclude on a broader scale that "a critique of SIBs is therefore more than a mere technical appraisal, but part of the necessary effort to rehumanise social policy and reclaim spheres of social life which should lie beyond the scope of the market" (Sinclair, McHugh and Roy 2021: 22).

Hybrid organizations (HOs) have been the subject of much recent discussion. A thorough systematic review of the literature and of the concept can be found in a recent article by Perobelli, Caparello and Saporito (2024). They define HOs the following way quoting Billis and Rochester (2020: 1): "Formal organizations that utilize the distinctly different principles of one of the three sectors (public, private, third)" (Perobelli, Cappellaro and Saporito 2024: 1). They view HOs as "a legacy of New Public Management". Later on they say that "HO's are primarily unitary organizations that govern the relationship between public and private spheres through formal governance mechanisms" (Perobelli, Cappellaro and Saporito 2024: 3). They suggest that the difference between a PPP and a HO is the theoretical lenses where they claim PPPs are studied through transaction costs theory while HOs are studied through organizational institutionalism. The main claim therefore seems to be that HOs are seen as formal organizations. Through their literature review, they identify 95 journal articles on HOs. Half of these articles concern state-owned enterprises which Perobelli et al. also classify as HOs and acknowledge the overlap in the literature.

Hybrid organizations have been mentioned before in the literature on public management and governance as this quote from Stephen Osborne in the concluding chapter of his edited volume on *The New Public Governance* attests to:

> Now the concept of hybrid is not a new one. There has been a longstanding debate about "publicness" in PSOs (public service organizations, ed.) and the blurring of the boundaries between public and private organizations. What is distinctive now is the growing complexity of this hybridity. It is not simple a blurring of the boundaries between public and private. Rather it is the evolution of genuinely new forms of organizational architecture that are not bound by sectoral limitations and that engender new forms of accountability.
>
> (Osborne 2009: 417)

Ecosystems are defined as:

> (…) a specific form of collaboration between government and non-government actors – such as private firm, not-for-profit organizations, citizens, and so on – that often rely on platforms orchestrated by the government where both public and non-public organizations and individuals could coexist and interact by developing complementary products and services.
>
> (Ysa, Schedler and Christòfol 2022: 330)

The key word to distinguish them from partnerships seems to be "platforms". Ecosystems are said to have the following characteristics: hybridity, informality, reciprocity, openness, regulation and orchestration, and public value (Ysa, Schedler and Christòfol 2022: 331–332). The authors call for more "empirical pilots" in order to find out what ecosystems are capable of.

Partnerships in the literature on public management

This section traces the recent development of the partnership concept in the public management literature.

The first stage concerned the development from New Public Management (NPM) to New Public Governance (NPG). NPM was all about management and markets (Hood 1991). The focus regarding the private sector was to contract out tasks to the private sector or to privatize in the sense of selling off shares in state-owned companies. It gradually became clear that a wholesale transition to new markets were not happening because of the nature of public tasks. Instead, what economists called "quasi-markets". It meant a lot more interaction between the public sector and the private sector.

The concept of governance captured the mood well, and the phrase governing without government came into fashion. Governance encompasses governing, but the government does not have to be in driver's seat all the time. The famous book on Reinventing Government (Osborne and Gaebler 1993) dubbed it steering, not rowing. Governance now meant a broader definition of governing where private sector actors were in a complex relationship with the private sector. The preferred mode of governance was the network – the relationship between many different organizations bound together by network ties. To capture this movement in the public management literature, Osborne (2009) coined the concept of the New Public Governance. It was still mainly concerned with public governance and was a governance paradigm as authors later described it (Torfing et al. 2020).

A literature grew up around the organizational aspect of this change from NPM to governance and NPM. Since not all activities could be fully privatized or merely contracted out, the complex co-operation between the public sector and the private sector took place in new forms of organizations – PPPs. The literature had two intertwined pedigrees. The broader public governance literature and the more specialized privatization literature on PPPs were seen as the new thing.

The PPP literature focused mostly, although not exclusively, the concrete organizational form of a PPP. The result was the five different organizational forms of a partnership mentioned above. This literature developed over the years. Hodge and Greve (2019, 2022) assembled a number of edited volumes where the partnership contributions could unfold. Scholarly debates occurred at IRSPM conferences and in a scholarly network called the IP3SN, International

Public-Private Partnership Scholarly Network during the 2010s (ending by 2020 because of Corona and it was not reinvigorated after that time).

Like with the privatization debate two decades earlier, much of the PPP dynamics empirically came out of the UK, due to both policy partnerships and infrastructure partnerships as a result of the British Private Finance Initiative policy. The UK experience became the focus of attention, although it soon turned out that there were dynamics in infrastructure partnerships going on in Australia, Canada, and the United States to name but a few countries. Today, partnerships are a global phenomenon.

A few scholars wrote both in the network/NPG branch of the literature and in the more specialized PPP literature. This included mainly Dutch scholars, especially Erik-Hans Klijn and Joop Koppenjan, and Stephen Osborne. Osborne coined the concept of NPG, but in 2001 he had edited one of the first volumes on PPPs.

The next development occurred when scholars began to embrace the concept of collaboration more widely. Collaboration as a concept had already been there for a while, but a number of public management scholars found the partnership term too focused on the organizational form, and the network concept too restricting in terms of identifying network ties, so a new debate focused on collaborative governance. These authors tried to widen the net to identify many types of collaborations. There were talks of collaborative regimes. Collaborative governance also got intertwined with the concept of public sector innovation and co-creation. The widening of the literature leads to calls for and attempts towards new form of synthesises.

John Bryson and Barbara Crosby and colleagues are among those with most success in creating synthesises out of close related literatures. Their articles on both collaboration and partnerships have been widely cited (see, for example, Bryson, Crosby and Middleton 2015), and they are also the ones that took most care in creating a carefully created synthesis. Together with various colleagues, they have incorporated many important aspects of the public management literature. This includes their highly successful merger of Moore's creating public value theory with the organizational forms of partnerships and then collaborative governance. Since then, their research team has discussed and adopted a number of new insights, including leading social movements and amberdexterity. The systems approach can be seen in this light as well.

The widening of the partnership approach got narrowed again when a new generation of researchers focused on hybrids as an organizational form between the public sector and the private sector. This was in conjunction with the increasing focus on grand challenges and wicked problems. The argument, as also previously presented, was that wicked problems cannot be solved by anyone organization alone and therefore necessitate collaboration between organizations from two or more sectors. The debate on hybrids also made it more likely that scholars from public management and organization studies would begin to speak more to each other and cite each other more often. The literature now sometimes refer to "hybrids" as the preferred term and sometimes to "partnerships" (see Gray, Purdy and Asari 2022 for the latter). Organizational scholars had long been interested in inter-organizational collaboration. The big difference was that the public management scholars would normally start from the premise that public managers needed to collaborate with someone in order to produce public value whereas organizational scholars could just as well be studying collaborations between private sector firms and NGOs.

In the scholarly landscape, there seems to be an interest in continuing to strive for synthesises or least some greater analytical frameworks that can be used to study a number of aspects in partnerships. This goes for the Quelin, Kivleniece and Lazzarine (2017) article, the works of Bryson and Crosby, and that of Eggers and Kettl, as well as for those that wants to study power in collaborative settings (Gray, Purdy and Ansari 2022). It seems as if the public governance aspects have been somewhat in the background, although it still exists, and NPG is well and doing fine as a concept. Perhaps the new overarching challenge of climate change, war in Europe, and inequality has sowed the seeds for a more common or mutual discussion on the continuing need for partnerships?

What are the controversies with partnerships about?

Partnerships are generally seen as a force of good, but there are also some controversies. Do partnerships get too exclusive so that outside actors are shut out of the action? This is especially a problem where there are rules of outsourcing, and partnerships may be seen as too closed a shop which create unfair competition. Another issue is that partnerships functions over longer time periods which makes it difficult to come up with quick results or produce public value immediately. Policy makers may therefore be hesitant to begin partnerships because they cannot see the immediate payoff. A related problem is that it then often takes too long time and becomes complicated to find out what type of value the partnership has produced. Then there is the accountability issue which has often plagued partnerships. Who exactly is accountable when many stakeholders have been active in the partnership? This is a severe problem when there is a breakdown in the relationship and when a blame game starts. Because many partners are working together, it becomes more difficult to pinpoint who had the responsibility if something went wrong. Researchers have tried to address many of these issues, as we shall see later on, but most of the controversies remain to this day. A separate chapter is devoted to partnership and democracy.

What are the burning issues that partnerships are occupied with contemporarily? First, there is the challenge from climate change. Obviously, this was addressed in the UN's SDGs and in the Paris Agreement. This is a super wicked issue by far and it demands collaborations from many partners. The Covid-19 crisis is another wicked issue that the world has been grappling with since March 2020 and where this light at the end of the tunnel in some countries finally. The migration issue is also something of a wicked problem, which calls for many organizations' actions. Cybercrime is an issue as well that demand many eyes on it, and so it is a fertile ground for making partnerships.

How are partnerships organized? They are typically formed as a temporary organization where the partners come together to work together on a particular topic of their concern. There is a continuum from more tight organizational structures to looser organizational structures that is widely recognized in the literature (Bryson, Crosby and Bloomberg 2015; O'Flynn and Wanna 2008). Keast (2016:36) distinguishes between a merger, an alliance, a joint venture, a network, a consortium, a coalition, and a partnership. To Keast, the partnership is a formal legal association for the purpose of shared profit/loss or an informal connecting relationship with the following defining features: unincorporated, smaller number of partners, linked by written (formal) contract or verbal (informal) contract, incomplete contracts and time limited by agreement. As the ANU Press volume from Butcher and Gilchrist says,

> Collaboration also needs an agreed framework for accountability and the management of risk (financial, legal, reputational and political). And above all, these frameworks need to "work" for each of the partners. It might not always be possible to achieve a neat fit with the internal policies and business systems used by partner organizations, and some forbearance and flexibility may be required.
>
> (Butcher and Gilchrist 2020: 84)

"Collaboration represents an attempt to work flexibly and adaptively in complex and uncertain systems" (p. 84). Risk is important and we can distinguish between a fail-safe policy and safe-fail policy. Start with a Terms of Reference and secure a memorandum of understanding.

Partnership is a way of thinking

It is not only a model. Partnership (or collaboration) is much more a way of thinking. You could almost say that collaboration is a mind-set. A best practice framework can be devised, which consists of the following elements (Butcher and Gilchrist 2020: 89).

- Purpose (work towards a common goal)
- Communication (encourage clear communication)
- Expectations (ensure that expectations and goals are aligned)

- Evidence (compile evidence about the partnership)
- Systems mapping
- Consult stakeholders and experts
- Authorising environment
- Executive leadership/backing
- Roles and contributions
- "Zippered" relationships
- Collaboration space
- Independent facilitation
- Governance
- Sustainability
- Conflict resolution
- Future proofing

The number one goal here is that "collaboration is about mobilizing people and organizations in support of an alternative approach so solving complex problems" (Butcher and Gilchrist 2020: 96). And leadership is about communication first and foremost when it comes to collaboration.

How to get to a partnership? Beth Simone Noveck (2021: 271–284) offers the following steps: (1) identifying clear value from the partnership, (2) identifying and recruiting prospective partners, (3) articulating the mission and defining roles, (4) designing the type of partnership, (5) articulating the theory of change, and (6) creating a governance structure.

The collective impact approach was developed by Kania and Kramer. They define collective impact as:

> Long-term commitments by a group of important actors from different sectors to a common agenda for solving a specific social problem. Their actions are supported by a shared measurement system, mutually reinforcing activities, and ongoing communication, and are staffed by an independent backbone organization.
>
> (Kania and Kramer 2011: 39)

The collective impact approach consists of a common agenda, shared measurement systems, mutually reinforcing activities, continuous communication, and a backbone support organization. But there remains an illusive ideal of a tangible impact.

Kania and Kramer's concept was a step forward for the practical world of partnerships when it was published in 2011. Kania and Kramer subsequently build a consultancy business around the concept. While many partnership texts and theories have flourished at the time, few scholars have explicated what a partnership organization might mean in practice. Kania and Kramer's five items seemed to make sense in that respect. Formulate a common agenda that partners can come together for. Agree on a shared measurement system that will record the progress of the partnership. Create mutually reinforcing activities that will keep the partners in contact with each other. There must be continuing communication to provide the basis for an ongoing dialogue. Finally, the existence of a backbone support organization. This has often been the missing link in many descriptions and analysis of partnerships, and Kania and Kramer highlighted the need for a solid backbone organization behind a working partnership.

Bardach (1998: 8) wrote: "I define collaboration as any joint activity by two or more agencies that is intended to increase public value by their working together rather than separately".

Bardach (1998) talked about objective and subjective components to collaboration. Objective components are formal agreements, personnel, and budgetary considerations. Subjective components are belief in the legitimacy and desirability of collaborative action, i.e. the readiness to act on this belief and trust in those whose co-operation is essential for success (ANU Press 2020) Chris Eccles has been head of the Victorian Department of Premier and Cabinet. We are moving to a future that is less siloed and portfolio-driven towards more reliance on collaboration, co-operation, and co-design according to Chris Eccles from Australia.

Bardach was one of earlier policy scholars to engage seriously with the concepts of partnerships and collaboration. Bardach produced various sought-after books and articles on the matter, and continued to contribute to the literature on collaboration. The points he made about the imperative for collaboration have been echoed many times since, and subject to interpretations and building on newer generations of scholars.

Donahue and Zeckhauser also feature prominently in the literature as serious scholars of collaboration and partnerships. Donanue and Zeckhauser (2011) preferred the concept of "collaborative governance" and were critical to the point of dismissing the "public-private partnership" concept in their 2011 book.

Donahue and Zeckhauser (2011: 4) used the following definition of collaborative governance: "carefully structured arrangements that interweave public and private capabilities on terms of shared discretion". In a rather optimistic perspective at the time, Donahue and Zeckhauser wrote:

> Collaborative governance harnesses all of America's capacity – public and private, for-profit and nonprofit, employee and volunteer – to the pursuit of the common good. And it unleashes the unpredictable resourcefulness of an entrepreneurial people to improvise fresh, flexible solutions. It encourages private engagement in public missions, and it optimistic – but not naive – about the potential for sharing responsibility while ensuring accountability.
>
> (Donahue and Zeckhauser 2011: 285)

Later, they have focused their energy on comparing how PPPs work in China and the United States (Eccleston, Donahue and Zeckhauser 2021).

The collaboration experience is therefore a mix of objective and subjective components, and to make it work the actors and institutions have to put in a combined effort.

For the leaders, Crosby and Bryson note that:

> A central challenge for leaders is to bring diverse stakeholders together in shared-power arrangements in which they can pool information, other resources, and activities around a common purpose. The focus should be on key stakeholders – those most affected by a social and need or public problem or who have important resources for meeting the need.
>
> (Crosby and Bryson quoted in Butcher and Gilchrist 2020: 7)

Partnership leaders are seen by bridgebuilders as they are called by Eggers and Kettl (2023, Chapter 5) and when they are managing a catalytic government, they can have the following qualities and tasks: (1) build dedicated scouting and sensing capabilities, (2) develop foresight abilities, (3) use the right tools to spur actions, (4) balance risk and returns, (5) reshape internal incentive structures. (6) tap into diverse perspectives across the network, (7) create markets to cultivate innovations, (8) identify the right player for each role across the innovation life cycle, (9) beware the "valley of death" (from small scale research funding to full-scale acquisition, and (10) align incentives to shared goals.

In this book, we will pursue a path of collaborative leadership thought that fit partnerships. It starts with the public manager as a boundary spanner and bridge builder. This is subsequently taken up by other authors. We then discuss Ansell and Gash's four categories of partnership managers. Attributes to managers have made by various authors as part of the more comprehensive models of partnerships and collaboration. The broader concept of boundary spanning was elaborated in a recent book. This leads us to the shared leadership approach that Bryson et al. where it is about leading social change from the principles of directing, aligning, and committing.

Structure of the book

This book identifies several moves that partnerships have been going through:

- A move towards policy partnerships in order to respond to grand challenges (other types of partnerships more trapped in the NPM era)
- A move from vague partnerships to specific partnerships with clear and ambitious purpose
- A move from individual leadership qualities to collective leadership responsibilities
- A move from risk sharing to search for better outcomes and better resources to secure public value
- A move from making governments responsible for initiating partnerships to creating more space for private sector initiatives? (witness the growth of

foundations, of ESG within private sector companies). Governments can take the initiative, but they don't have to take the initiative.

The book is structured the following way:

- **Chapter 2** deals with who the managers of partnerships are and what they do.
- **Chapter 3** focuses on partnerships in the health sector.
- **Chapter 4** examines partnerships in smart cities.
- **Chapter 5** analyses partnerships for the climate.
- **Chapter 6** makes a case for partnerships and discusses democratic issues with partnerships.

Discussion questions

1 What elements of the definitions of a PPP do you believe are the most important ones and why?
2 Do the different types of PPPs mentioned in the chapter also exist in your country? Why are there more examples of one type of partnership than other types of partnerships?
3 What are the dynamics behind "the policy state" and "wicked problems" and how does it create the conditions for more partnerships or less partnerships in your assessment?

References

Alford, John & Brian Head. 2017. "Wicked and Less Wicked Problems: A Typology and a Contingency Framework" *Policy & Society* 36(3), 397–413.

Alonso, José M. & Rhys Andrews. 2022. "Can Public-Private Innovation Partnerships Improve Public Services? Evidence from a Synthetic Control Approach" *Public Administration Review* 82(6), 1138–1153.

Bardach, Eugene. 1998. *Getting Agencies to Work Together: The Practice and Theory of Managerial Craftmanship*. Washington, DC: Brookings.

Billis, David & Colin Rochester. Eds. 2020. *Handbook on Hybrid Organizations*. Chelthenham: Edward Elgar Publishing.

Bozeman, Barry. 2007. *Public Values and Public Interest: Counterbalancing Economic Individualism*. Washington, DC: Georgetown University Press.

Brewer, Gene. 2025. "Public and Private Values: A Continuing Story" in Hodge, Graeme; Greve, Carsten & Reeves, Eoin. Eds. *Research Handbook on Privatisation*. Cheltenham: Edward Elgar, pp. 193–212.

Brinkerhoff, Derick W. & Jenifer M. Brinkerhoff. 2011. "Public-Private Partnerships: Perspectives on Purposes, Publicness and Good Governance" *Public Administration and Development* 31, 2–14.

Brogaard, Lene. 2017. "The Impact of Innovation Training on Successful Outcomes in Public-Private Partnerships" *Public Management Review* 19(8), 1184–1205.

Brogaard, Lene. 2021. "Innovative Outcomes in Innovation Public-Private Partnerships: A Systematic Review of Empirical Evidence and Current Challenges" *Public Management Review* 23(1), 135–157.

Brogaard, Lene & Ole Helby Petersen. 2018. "Public-Private Partnerships (PPPs) in Development Policy: Exploring the Concept and Practice" *Development Policy Review* 36(2), 0729–0747.

Brown, Trevor; Matthew Potoski & David M. Van Slyke. 2013. *Complex Contracting. Government Purchasing of the US Coast Guard's Deepwater Program*. Cambridge, MA: Cambridge University Press.

Bryson, John; Barbara Crosby; Melissa Stone. 2006. "The Design and Implementation of Cross-Sector Collaboration: Propositions from the literature. Special issue. *Public Administration Review* 66, 44–55.

Bryson, John M.; Barbara Crosby & Laura Bloomberg. Eds. 2015. *Public Value and Public Administration*. Washington, DC: Georgetown University Press.

Bryson, John; Barbara Crosby & Melissa Middleton Stone. 2015. "The Design and Implementation of Cross-Sector Collaborations: Needed and Challenging" *Public Administration Review* 75(5), 647–663.

Bundgaard, Lasse. 2021. *Public-Private Innovation Partnerships: Creating Public Value and Scaling Up Sustainable City Solutions*. PhD thesis, Copenhagen Business School.

Butcher, John & David Gilchrist. 2020. *Collaboration for Impact: Lessons from the field*. Canberra: ANU Press.

Clarke, Amelia & Andrew Crane. 2018. "Cross-sector Partnerships for Systemic Change: Systematized Literature Review and Agenda for Further Research" *Journal of Business Ethics* 150; 303–313.

Donahue, John & Richard Zeckhauser. 2011. *Collaborative Governance*. Princeton, NJ: Princeton University Press.

Eccleston, Karen; John Donahue & Richard Zeckhauser. 2021. *The Dragon, the Eagle and the Private Sector. Public-Private Collaboration in China and in the United States*. Cambridge: Cambridge University.

Eggers, William & Donald F. Kettl. 2023. *Bridgebuilders: How Governments can Transcend Boundaries to Solve Big Problems*. Boston, MA: Harvard Business Review Press.

Forrer, John; James Edwin Kee & Eric Boyer. 2015. *Governing Cross-Sector Collaboration*. San Francisco, CA: Jossey-Bass.

Gray, Barbara; Jill Purdy & Shahzad Ansari. 2022. "Confronting Power Asymmetries in Partnerships to Address Grand Challenges" *Organization Theory* 3, 1–25.

Greve, Carsten & Tamyko Ysa. Eds. 2023. *Handbook on Strategic Public Management*. Cheltenham: Edward Elgar.

Hodge, Graeme A. & Carsten Greve. 2019. *The Logic of Public-Private Partnerships: The Enduring Interdependency of Politics and Markets*. Cheltenham: Edward Elgar.

Hodge, Graeme A. & Carsten Greve. Eds. 2022. *A Research Agenda for Public-Private Partnerships and the Governance of Infrastructure*. Cheltenham: Edward Elgar.

Hood, Christopher. 1991. "A Public Management for All Seasons" *Public Administration* Spring, 3–19.

Kania, John & Mark Kramer. 2011. "Collective Impact" *Stanford Social Innovation Review* Winter 2011, 36–41.

Keast, Robyn. 2016, "Integration terms: Same or different?", in Carrey, Gemma. Ed., Grassroots to government: *Creating joined-up working in Australia, Melbourne: Melbourne* University Press, pp. 27–42.

Kekez, Anka; Michael Howlett & Michael Ramesh. 2018. "Varieties of Collaboration in Public Service Delivery" *Policy Design and Practice* 1(4), 243–252.

Kettl, Donald F. 1993. *Sharing Power. Public Governance and Private Markets*. Washington, DC: Brookings.

Klijn, Erik-Hans & Geert Teisman. 2003. "Institutional and Strategic Barriers to Public-Private Partnerships" *Public Money & Management* 23(3), 137–146.

Klijn, Erik-Hans. 2022. "Theories of Public-Private Partnerships" in Hodge, Graeme & Greve, Carsten. Eds. *A Research Agenda for Public-Private Partnerships and the Governance of Infrastructure*. Cheltenham: Edward Elgar, pp. 33–52.

McQuaid, Ronald W. 2009. "Theory of Organizational Partnership Advantages, Disadvantages and Success Factors" in Osborne, Stephen. Ed. *The New Public Governance?* London: Routledge, pp. 127–148.

Moore, Mark. 1995. *Creating Public Value*. Cambridge, MA: Harvard University Press.

Moore, Mark. 2013. *Recognizing Public Value*. Cambridge, MA: Harvard University Press.

Noveck, Beth S. 2021. *Solving Public Problems*. New Haven, CT: Yale University Press.

O'Flynn, Janine & John Wanna. Eds. 2008 *Collaborative Governance*. Canberra: ANU Press.

Orren, Karen & Stephen Skowronek. 2017. *The Policy State. An American Predicament*. Cambridge, MA: Harvard University Press.

Osborne, David & Gaebler Ted. 1993. *Reinventing Government*. New York: Plume.

Osborne, Stephen. 2009. "Conclusions: Public Governance and Public Services Delivery: A Research Agenda for the Future" in Osborne, Stephen. Ed. *The New Public Governance?* London: Routledge, pp. 413–428.

Page, Stephen B. & Melissa M. Stone. 2023. "Collaborative Architecture: Components, Relationships, and Implications for Partner Influence" *Perspectives on Public Management and Governance* 6(1), 14–27.

Perobelli, Eleonora; Giulia Cappellaro & Raffella Saporito. 2024. "Public-Private Hybrid Organizations in the Public Sector: Evidence and Future Directions from a Systematic Literature Review" *Public Management Review* 27(11), 1–28.

Quelin, Betrand; Ilze Kivleniece & Sergio Lazzarine. 2017. "Public-Private Collaboration, Hybridity and Social Value: Towards New Theoretical Perspectives" *Journal of Management Studies* 54(6), 763–792.

Roberts, Alasdair. 2020. "The Third and Fatal Shock: How Pandemic Killed the Millennial Paradigm" *Public Administrative Review* 80(4), 603–609.

Sancino, Alessandro. 2022. *Public Value Co-Creation: A Multi-Actor and Multi-Sector Perspective*. Emerald Publishing. Bingley, UK.

Sinclair, Rob; Neil McHugh & Michael J. Roy. 2021. "Social Innovation, Financialisation, and Commodification: A Critique of Social Bonds" *Journal of Economic Policy Reform* 24(1), 11–27.

Sullivan, Helen & Chris Skelcher. 2002. Working *Across Boundaries in Public Services*. London: PalgraveMacMillan.

Sullivan, Helen; Paul Williams; Stephen Jeffares. 2012. "Leadership for Collaboration Situated agency in practice" *Public Administration Review* 14, 41–66.

Sullivan, Helen. 2022. *Collaboration and Public Policy*. London: Palgrave MacMillan.

Torfing, Jacob; Lotte Bøgh Andersen; Carsten Greve & Kurt K. Klausen. 2020. *Public Governance Paradigms*. Cheltenham: Edward Elgar.

Vaillancourt Rosenau, Pauline. 1999. "Introduction: The Strengths and Weaknesses of Public-Private Policy Partnerships" *The American Behavioural Scientist* 43(1), 10–34.

Wilson, Rob; Alec Fraser; Jonathan Kimmitt; Stefanie Tan; Neil McHugh; Toby Lowe; Mildred Warner; Susan Baines & Eleanor Carter. 2020. "Editorial: Whither Social Impact Bonds (SIBs)? The Future of Social Investment. Theme: Futures in Social Investment? Learning from the Emerging Policy and Practice of Social Impact Bonds" *Public Money & Management* 40(3), 179–182.

Winther, Sigge Nielsen. 2025. *The Puzzle State: How to Govern Wicked Problems in Western Democracies*. Copenhagen: Gad Publishers.

Ysa, Tamyko; Kuno Schedler & Conill Christòfol. 2022. "Ecosystems in a Government Context" in Schedler, Kuno. Ed. *Elgar Encyclopedia of Public Management*. Cheltenham: Edward Elgar, pp. 330–334.

Selected readings

Bryson, John; Barbara Crosby & Melissa M. Stone. 2015. "The Design and Implementation of Cross-Sector Collaborations: Needed and Challenging" *Public Administration Review* 75(5), 647–663.

The classic article that enlists almost every aspect you want to know about public-private partnerships and collaboration. The article addresses the different elements that go into a collaborative partnership in a systematic and convincing way. The model Bryson and colleagues present is still one of the most clear-sighted and relevant models of a collaborative partnership available.

Orren, Karen & Stephen Skowronek. 2017. *The Policy State. An American Predicament*. Cambridge, MA: Harvard University Press.

Delivers a compelling argument for the policy context that partnerships take place in. Explains how the surge to make policy and be solution-oriented provides fertile ground for new ways of organizing, including partnerships. Although mainly U.S.-oriented, the lesson applies to many other countries as well where problem-solving and the prevalence of policy exist.

Quelin, Betrand; Ilze Kivleniece & Sergio Lazzarine. 2017. "Public-Private Collaboration, Hybridity and Social Value: Towards New Theoretical Perspectives" *Journal of Management Studies* 54(6), 763–792.

Provides an excellent overview of the many debates on public-private partnerships and collaborations and makes an attempt at providing a synthesis of the many discussions. It is written from an organizational point of view that incorporates both the private sector and the public sector perspective.

2 The public manager as partnership manager

From boundary spanners to bridgebuilders in collective leadership contexts

Learning objectives

By the end of this chapter, you should:

- Have a sense of why the role of the partnership manager is important in partnerships
- Get an impression of the way the literature on partnership managers have developed
- Get closer to the roles of the partnership manager

Key points of this chapter

- The role of the partnership manager has been singled out as one of the most important elements in making partnerships work in practice.
- There have been different stages in the research on partnership managers that also borrow from theories of governance networks and collaboration more generally.
- Today, there are now a variety of activities and expectations associated with being a manager of a partnership.

Key terms

- The role of the partnership manager is linked to a number of balancing acts that make a partnership function in practice.

DOI: 10.4324/9781003020844-2

- Metaphors range from being a juggler and a boundary spanner to being a bridgebuilder.
- Today, a partnership manager is a complex one, embedded in a larger context of collective leadership.

Introduction

This chapter examines the role of the individual public manager in the new role of a partnership manager. A number of recent descriptions have been added recently to the undertakings public managers perform when they manage partnerships. A "playmaker" was how a public manager dealing with social issues described herself in a public management class recently.

This chapter presents the most used terms used to characterize this new role. These include: the boundary spanner (launched by Williams and followed up by others), Ansell and Gash's three roles, the leadership tasks involved in managing a collaborative effort, and the most recent focus on leading a social transformation and collective leadership.

The partnership manager is perhaps the most important actor in any partnership. Or should we way partnership management, because it does not necessarily have to be one individual, but there is capacity for managing a partnership can be shared as the approach to collective leadership implies. As Crosby et.al. (2009: 200) once said: "We see the leadership practice of these leaders as integrative – that is, they help organizations integrate people, processes, structures and resources in semi-permanent ways". And they continue:

> Collaborations are unlikely to get very far (…) unless partners develop enough trust to continue working together and find ways to deal with power imbalances, coping with shifting membership, develop supportive processes and structures and have a system of evaluating outcomes and fostering accountability (…).
>
> (Crosby et.al. 2009: 203)

When some action or implementation of policy is carried out by partnerships it is the acknowledgement that more actors are needed than a single organization: "Emphasizing an era of governance implies that implementation action involves a multiplicity of actors contributing to the results of public programmes rather than merely the 'lonely organization' (Hjern 1982) assumed in some early studies" (O'Toole and Meier 2009: 323).

Vangen and Huxham (2009) developed a theory on collaborative advantage, defined as "the synergy that can be created through joint working" (Vangen and Huxham 2009: 163). They also point to a possible outcome called collaborative inertia: "the tendency for collaborative activities to be frustratingly show to produce output or unconformtably conflict-ridden" (Vangen and Huxham 2009: 163). Vangen and Huxham acknowledge what they refer to as "managerial tensions" in collaborative settings like partnerships: misaligned expectations vs. sophisticated stereotyping, cultural sensitive versus generic communication, flexibility versus established organizational procedures, autonomy versus accountability, and retaining control versus grappling with complexity (Vangen and Huxham 2009: 174). Vangen and Huxham (2009: 178–180) contends at one point that "Leadership is likely to be beyond the scope of any one individual to tackle, and leadership activities are likely to incorporate dilemmas of ideology and pragmatism". What can then be considered a success in a partnership? Vangen and Huxham believe that there are five types of successes that can be attributed to a partnership: (1) substantive outcomes; (2) success related to the process of collaborating; (3) emergent or semi-serendipitous achievements, i.e. new results that were not planned or thought of in advance; (4) recognition or acknowledgement of the partnership by those not directly involved in the partnership or though the request of providing consultancy expertise to a similar, but new type of partnership elsewhere; (5) personal pride by the people who have been involved in the partnership. Being part of something that is recognized as "a job well done" (Vangen and Huxham 2009: 180–181) is important for a partnership to have reached a milestone (Vangen and Huxham 2009: 181–182).

The story of PPPs is also the story of the partnership manager. In the literature it has been told many times that the partnership manager is someone who juggles different roles and expectations. In many ways it is the same that people say about middle managers. And managers of partnerships are really in the middle. They are in the middle of two and more other organizations from the public sector and the private sector where the private sector consists of both for-profit companies and non-government organizations or voluntary organizations. They are the ones who must drive the partnership forward and to a certain extent be visionary leaders, and they are also the ones who should build bridges to other organization.

One point of discussion, as hinted to previously, is whether all responsibility should be place upon the shoulder of one leader – the partnership manager – or is indeed a broader responsibility that more people must share – partnership management. Huxham and Vangen seem to think that it will be a collective responsibility and here they are in tune with the more recent literature on collective leadership. Others seem to talk about the leaders' capacities, and this could perhaps include Eggers and Kettl in their presentation of the bridgebuilder.

If a partnership involves a portfolio or eco-systems of partnerships, the role of managing partnerships might change and John Bryson and colleagues have written about when they talk of strategic management-at-scale. Strategy management-at-scale can have two approaches: the collective impact approach or the community organizing, coalition building and advocacy. This has consequences for leadership:

> Strategy management-at-scale requires effective leadership, but how? Strikingly little attention is paid to the actual strategizing efforts of leaders of various kinds in the public and nonprofit literature; what attention exists is seldom informed by a theoretical understanding of strategy, strategizing and strategic management.
>
> (Bryson, Crosby & Barberg 2023: 106–107)

Bryson et al. proposes to go with the "Direction-Alignment-Commitment" framework that the Center for Creative Leadership has formulated.

But the scale-issue will certainly be of increasing importance in the future:

> (…) we believe it is important to take seriously to develop the field of strategy management-at-scale because to many of the major challenges the world faces require multi-actor, multi-organization, cross-sector responses.
>
> (Bryson, Crosby & Barberg 2023)

The boundary spanner

The American public policy scholar, Eugene Bardach, has said that "whatever else might help explain success in the collaborative process, the efforts and creativity of what I call purposive practitioners is an essential explanatory ingredient" (Bardach in Williams 2012: 196).

Williams writes that a boundary spanner should be thought of as a networker, an entrepreneur, and an innovator, as the ability to engage with others shows high trust with a special kind of personality and traits as a leader. The personality is said to see the boundary spanner as someone being personable, respectful, tolerant, diplomatic, caring, and commanding. Catalytic leaders assume the characteristics of thinking and acting strategically and have interpersonal skills for facilitating a productive working group or network and underlying character. They are also seen as integrators, diplomats, cross-fertilizers, and deep-thinkers (see also Williams 2002, 2011, 2019).

Williams found that the following characteristics were pertinent to effective collaborative working: (1) building sustainable relationships which involved communicating and listening, understanding, emphasizing and resolving conflict, personality, and trust; (2) managing through influencing and negotiation which involves networking; (3) managing complexity and interdependences; and (4) managing roles, accountabilities, and motivations. The managing of multiple accountabilities is a key task for a boundary spanner.

As Williams acknowledges, the boundary spanner is a network manager that builds personal relationships with a wide range of other actors and have the ability to manage in a non-hierarchical decision environment through negotiation and brokering. The boundary spanner connects problems to solutions and mobilizes resources and effort to produce public value. A recent empirical study on boundary spanners in the National Health Service explores the possibility of boundary spanners to make a difference (Alexander 2024).

Writing about the boundary spanner, Helen Sullivan (2022) remarked that Williams (2012) identified the capacity to have the ability to appreciate and analyse connections, links and interrelationships, and that also understanding contexts and conditions of collaboration is important. Sullivan suggests that Williams' characterization of boundary spanning activities, including making connections, is now integrated and commonplace in a lot of professional public management activities today. This happens after news of NPM and NPG.

Sullivan (2022) also notes that in a world of wicked problems, a boundary spanner's work is less to provide neat solutions, but to keep at connecting people to attend to the problems at hand on a continuing basis:

> The emphasis is not here on achieving a goal (i.e. "solve" a wicked problem) but maintaining a level of endeavour that respects the significance of the challenge but also is cognizant of the inadequacy of existing capacity to respond, including relevant expertise.
>
> (Sullivan 2022)

Ansell and Gash (2018, 2012) identified three main roles for public managers in collaborative settings. They write that leadership is often the residual category and that the adjective usually associated with collaboration is "facilitate". This supports the movement towards distributed leadership where leadership is for the common good as Bryson and Crosby formulated it. The three roles described by Ansell and Gash are steward, mediator, and catalyst. A steward is someone who establishes and protects the integrity of the collaboration process. A mediator is someone who arbitrates and nurtures relationships between stakeholders. A catalyst is someone who identifies opportunities for creating value and mobilizes supporters.

Morse (2010) talked about "integrative leadership" to produce public value. Morse stated that

> The collective idea is more than an abstract idea. It is a common purpose, a common vision that unites those that created it and motivates them to act together to achieve it. Integration, in its ideal form, is more than cooperating to meet one's own ends (…) Since Follett's time (Mary Parker Follett, ed.) the core idea behind integration has gained currency in popular conceptions of management and leadership. The notions "win/win" and "synergy", for example, are very much rooted in Follett's formulation of integration (…).
>
> (Morse 2010: 232)

Morse (2010) elaborates:

> Integrative public leadership then is not a about private ends being met through collaboration, nor is it about the public sector co-opting other actors to achieve organizational goals. Rather it is about the process through which multiple actors with multiple interests create a common vision of, and work together to create public value (i.e. the common good or the public interest).

Meerkerk and Edelenbos (2018a) focus on the boundary spanner's effort to facilitate relationship-building and creating commitment among network actors. This includes being able to "creating an environment in which representatives of organizations with different interests and perceptions become more willing to cross organizational, professional and/or social boundaries and invest in boundary-spanning activities". They therefore hypnotize that "a facilitative management style will foster boundary-spanning activity in the governance network". The other issue they focus on is that "a higher level of executive support will foster boundary-spanning activity".

They conclude that:

> facilitative management is an important stimulating condition for triggering boundary spanning activity in governance networks. A facilitative project management style, which accepts and not reduces the complexity of stakeholder environments is focused on informal relationship building and looks for ways to empower the stakeholder environment in defining, preparing and implementing the project, evokes boundary-spanning activity of network actors from these stakeholder environments.
>
> (Van Meerkerk and Edelenbos 2018a)

They also note that:

> executive support is important for fostering a facilitative management style. A principal who is committed but gives room for project management to enact a facilitative and open management style in this respect indirectly contributes to a context in which boundary-spanning activity of network actors is more likely to emerge.
>
> (Van Meerkerk and Edelenbos 2018a: 521)

Van Meerkerk and Edelenbos (2018b) have more in the book on the boundary spanning phenomenon: boundary spanning in public management and governance. They identify four roles for boundary spanners in this book: relational, coordination, mediation, and entrepreneurship. There are four main profiles: fixer, bridger, broker, and innovator/entrepreneur. Four main factors determine boundary spanning behaviour: individual determinants that relate to the competencies and capacities of individual actors; environmental features that define structure; role definitions and stressors; and organizational support and feedback.

The bridgebuilder

Bryson et al. talk about leading a social transformation in their latest article from 2021. The mindset for this, which they take from Kania, includes: getting all the right eyes on the problem, understanding that relational is as important as the rational, understanding structure is as important as strategy, sharing credit is important as taking credit, paying attention to adaptive work and not just technical solutions.

The leadership qualities that Bryson et al. associate with leading social transformations are focused on: collaboration skills; organizing and mobilizing ability; shared visualization, strategy mapping and visually assisted strategy management; skilled facilitation; storytelling about humans embedded in complex adaptive systems; broadly based coalition building and advocacy.

Eggers and Kettl (2023) focus on bridge-builders.

Eggers and Kettl identify ten ways to proceed for bridgebuilding: (1) knock down barriers, (2) seek mutual advantage, (3) nurture private partners, (4) build trustworthy networks, (5) grow catalytic government, (6) focus on outcomes, (7) make data the language, (8) redefine accountability, (9) cultivate cross-boundary leaders, and (10) make the exceptional routine.

For bridgebuilders at leaders: (1) create a common vision, (2) identify a cross-sector translator to lead the effort, (3) shift to collaborative governance, (4) empower team members, and (5) demonstrate empathy and understanding.

Further, across the network: (6) understand and leverage individual strengths, (7) build capabilities around skills rather than authority, (8) equip partners to tell powerful stories, (9) pay attention to social relationships, and (10) cultivate flexible, adaptable networks.

The ten ways bridgebuilders can scale bridgebuilding know-how across government are: (1) spur innovative solutions to wicked problems, (2) build government careers around bridgebuilding, (3) make it easier to move in and out of government, (4) break down internal silos, (5) channel resources toward intentional relationship building. And across networks: (6) tackle wicked problems as a team sport, (7) understand the system you are trying to change, (8) identify the highest leverage points to drive change, (9) identify a pool of interventions, (10) tap into each partners' "superpower".

Collective leadership and labs

Ospina et al. (2020) see collective dimensions of leadership as follows: (1) plural forms of leadership and leadership that reside in interpersonal relationships, (2) leadership that resides in systemic dynamics, (3) a theoretical lens and leadership in interpersonal relationships, and (4) a theoretical lens and leadership that resides in systemic dynamics.

Empson and Alvehus (2020) focus on collective leadership:

> In the past decade the study of leadership has moved beyond heroic, trait-based studies of individuals in conventional hierarchical organizations (…) to explore this phenomenon of collective leadership. Scholars focus on shared interaction in leadership processes. Concrete studies have focused on leadership dyads, triads and other forms of constellations.

Collective leadership is preoccupied with "collaborations among multiple individuals in formal and informal leadership positions" (Empson, Langley and Sergi 2023: 202). The literature views the relationship between collective leadership and individual leadership in the following way: (1) collective and individual leadership as oppositional, (2) collective and individual leadership as hybridized in organizational practices, and (3) collective and individual leadership as dialectic tension expressed through narratives.

Empson, Langley, and Sergi identify multiple archetypes of leaders, from a centripetal and a centrifugal dynamics. They find that "individuals committed to collective leadership nevertheless construct a single individual leader identity (the avatar) to embody the collective" (Empson, Langley and Sergi 2023: 221). "Individual and collective leadership narratives can co-exist and may even by mutually constitutive" (Empson, Langley and Sergi 2023: 221).

Empson, Langley, and Sergi conclude that:

> Our study reveals that through narratives, practitioners are able to accommodate a remarkable degree of ambiguity within their notions of leadership. Their ability to articulate a strong individual leader identity while professing commitment to an organizational narrative of collective leadership is not a sign of confusion. On the contrary, it exposes practitioners' complex and delicate narrative work, by which they accommodate centered and decentered conceptions of leadership.
>
> (Empson, Langley and Sergi 2023: 222)

Maybe partnership managers can learn something from the public narrative perspective developed by Ganz et al. (2023)? The public narrative approach sets out three phases: the story of self, the story of us, and the story of now. Partnership managers can talk about what motivates them to become engaged in partnerships. This could be their own story on how they came to be heading a partnership instead of another type of organization. Then there is "the story of us" which could be the story of the partnership's development itself. How did the partnership come into being? What spurred on the initial groundwork for establishing the partnership? The next phase in the public narrative is "the story of now". Why is the partnership important to have in the world right now? What is it that makes this particular partnership to compelling? The story of a partnership can be an integral part of the conditions for managing a partnership. One example could be the Danish Wholegrain Partnership. The partnership manager was motivated by working with different people and had a career in marketing. There was a need for a community for wholegrain products more generally. And the story of now is that eating more wholegrain products can benefit the health of the whole population.

Labs

Another way to look at how public managers promote their thoughts on public value creation in partnerships is through the recent institution of a lab. These are variously called policy labs or public service innovation labs. These labs have sprung up during the last decade in many countries worldwide. They are often funded by governments, yet able to have their own organizational space. Their main task is to provide alternatives and experiments to the usual way policy is made and administration is taken care of. They often encourage innovative thinking and experimentation. A number of labs are organized around human-centred design thinking (Bason 2023). Design thinking involves prototyping and other areas of experimentation. The professional staff comes from different educational backgrounds, including designers and anthropologists. They often stand in contrast to the more traditionally trained staff in government made up of people with a law degree, an economist degree, or a degree in political science and public policy.

MindLab in Denmark was one of the first and the most well-known policy labs. MindLab ceased to exist in 2018 after the Danish government had other priorities. While it was alive, MindLab championed design thinking in government. It buzzled with experiments. MindLab let ethnographic interventions and observations guide much of its work. MindLab was led by Christian Bason who later went on to advance design thinking in another government organization, the Danish Design Center.

MindLab was one of many policy labs around the world. An Australian survey found X = 52 number of policy labs working in Australia and New Zealand (Blomkamp and Lewis 2023: 147). There are policy labs in the UK, like the Nudge unit within government that was influential for a number of years. In the United States, the federal administration has initiated policy labs. Some of the more well-known ones include the Governance Lab led by Beth Simone Noveck. She just published a book on "Solving Public Problems" that builds on the work done by the Governance Lab (Noveck 2022). These are all policy labs that contribute with solutions to public issues and address wicked problems.

The policy labs have been able to demonstrate some success in influencing the public and political agenda on how to develop the public sector. The approach that design thinking brings to the table has in many ways been a fresh input into the public management reform context. Not many public organizations knew about human centred design thinking before. They do now and many local initiatives are also emerging that takes the message of design thinking to heart.

There are some debates as to how much influence human-centred design thinking in labs can have. As indicated above, some view it as a new and vigorous approach to public management reform and a type of thinking that will unleash more innovative activity in public sector organizations and make connections to private sector organizations in partnerships. Some view human-centred design thinking in labs as an extension of earlier times' optimism about designing public policies and institutions Others view it with more sceptical eyes, and point out that design thinking is focused on the "front end" of public policy making while not taking responsibility for the implementation process that comes after ideas have been generated and agreed upon.

Conclusion

This chapter has examined the development of the partnership manager in PPPs. The chapter has documented an evolution from the individual partnership manager as a boundary spanner to the bridgebuilder and most recently the partnership manager's role in collective leadership and design labs for policy.

Discussion questions

1. What are the primary characteristics of the public manager as partnership manager as you see them?
2. How has the role of the partnership manager evolved, and to what extent does it resemble collective leadership today?
3. What opportunities are there for partnership managers to make a difference on stakeholders in the organizational environment?

References

Alexander, James Duncan. 2024. "Public-Private Partnerships, Boundary Spanners and the Boundary Wall in the English National Health Service" *Journal of Health Organization and Management* 38(5), 662–681.

Ansell, Christopher & Alson Gash. 2012. "Stewards, Mediators and Catalysts: Toward a Model of Collaborative Leadership" *The Innovation Journal* 17(1), article 7.

Ansell, Christopher & Alison Gash. 2018. "Collaborative Governance as Practice Strategy" *Journal of Public Administration Research and Theory* 28(1), 16–32.

Bason, Christian. 2023. "Cross-fertilisation of Design Labs and Strategic Public Management" in Greve, Carsten and Ysa, Tamyko. Eds. *Handbook on Strategic Public Management*. Cheltenham: Edward Elgar 133–146.

Blomkamp, Emma & Jenny Lewis. 2023. "Magic PILs to Cure the Ills of Public Management? The Rise of Public Innovation Labs as Design-for-Policy Entrepreneurs" in Greve, Carsten & Tamyko Ysa. Eds. *Handbook on Strategic Public Management*. Chelthenham: Edward Elgar, 147–164

Bryson, John M.; Barbara Crosby & Bill Barberg. 2023. "Public Value Governance and Strategic Public Management" in Greve, Carsten and Ysa, Tamyko. Eds. *Handbook on Strategic Public Management*. Cheltenham: Edward Elgar, pp. 92–113.

Crosby, Barbara; John Bryson & Meilissa M. Stone. 2009. "Leading Across Frontiers: How Visionary Leaders Integrate People, Processes, Structures and Resources" in Osborne, Stephen. Ed. *The New Public Governance?* London: Routledge, pp. 200–222.

Eggers, William & Donald F. Kettl. 2023. *Bridgebuilders. How Government can Transcend Boundaries to Solve Big Problems*. Cambridge, MA: Harvard University Press.

Empson, Laura & Johan Alvehus. 2020. "Collective Leadership Dynamics among Professional Peers: Co-constructing an Unstable Equilibrium" *Organization Studies* 41(9), 1234–1256.

Empson, Laura; Ann Langley & Viviane Sergi. 2023. "When Everyone and No One is a Leader: Constructing Individual Leadership Identities while Sustaining an Organizational Narrative of Collective Leadership" *Organization Studies* 44(2), 201–277.

Ganz, Marshall; Julia Lee Cunningham; Inbal Ben Ezer & Alaina Segura. 2023. "Crafting Public Narrative to Enable Collective Action: A Pedagogy for Leadership Development" *Academy of Management Learning & Education* 22(2), 169–190.

Hjern, Benny. 1982. "Implementation Research - the link gone missing" *Journal of Public Policy*, 2: 301–308

Morse, Richard. 2010. "Integrative Public Leadership: Catalyzing Collaboration to Create Public Value" *The Leadership Quarterly* 21(2), 231–245.

Noveck, Beth S. 2022. *Solving Public Problems*. New Haven, CT: Yale University Press.

Ospina, Sonia; Erica G. Foldy; Gail T. Fairhust & Brad Jackson. 2020. "Collective Dimensions of Leadership: Connecting Theory and Method" *Human Relations* 73(4), 441–463.

O'Toole, Laurence Jr. & Kenneth J. Meier. 2009. "Implementation and Managerial Networking in the New Public Governance" in Osborne, Stephen. Ed. *The New Public Governance?* London: Routledge, pp. 322–336.

Sullivan, Helen. 2022. *Collaboration and Public Policy*. London: Palgrave MacMillan.

Williams, Paul. 2002. "The Competent Boundary Spanner" *Public Administration* 80(1), 103–124.

Williams, Paul. 2011. "The Life and Times of the Boundary Spanner" *Journal of Integrated Care* 19(3), 26–33.

Williams, Paul. 2012. *Collaboration in Public Policy and Practice: Perspectives on Boundary Spanners*. Bristol: Policy Press.

Williams, Paul. 2019. *Middle Managers as Agents of Collaboration*. Bristol: Bristol University Press.

Van Meerkerk, Ingmar & Jurian Edelenbos. 2018a. "Facilitating Conditions for Boundary Spanning Behaviour in Government Networks" *Public Management Review* 20(4), 503–524.

Van Meerkerk, Ingmar & Jurian Edelenbos. 2018b. *Boundary Spanners in Public Management and Governance: An Interdisciplinary Assessment.* Cheltenham: Edward Elgar.

Vangen, Siv & Chris Huxham. 2009. "Introducing the Theory of Collaborative Advantage" in Osborne, Stephen. Ed. *The New Public Governance?* London: Routledge, pp. 163–184.

Selected readings

Eggers, William & Kettl, Donald F. 2023. *Bridgebuilders. How Government can Transcend Boundaries to Solve Big Problems.* Cambridge, MA: Harvard University Press.

This is perhaps the most comprehensive and compelling overview of what partnership managers – what they call "bridgebuilders" – must be capable of in managing and leading complex partnerships. The book both provides an overview of the recent literature as well as offering some very hands-on advice for partnerships managers.

Van Meerkerk, Ingmar & Jurian Edelenbos. 2018. *Boundary Spanners in Public Management and Governance: An Interdisciplinary Assessment.* Cheltenham: Edward Elgar.

A comprehensive overview of the role of "the boundary spanner" that takes on such an important role in public-private partnerships as well as in other areas of public management and governance. Meerkerk and Edelelbos' volume brings together both new theoretical insights as well as empirical illustrations.

Noveck, Beth S. 2022. *Solving Public Problems.* New Haven, CT: Yale University Press.

Beth Simone Noveck brings a fresh perspective to the active and engaging role that managers can play in today's complex world and offers insights from practice as well as inspiration from a number of different types of partnerships than deals with wicked problems and grand challenges.

3 Partnerships in the health sector

Learning objectives

By the end of this chapter you should:

- Be clear about how partnerships can be of help in the health sector
- Get an understanding of which issues in healthcare are suitable for partnerships
- Be familiar with various empirical investigations into how partnerships in healthcare works

Key points of this chapter

- Partnerships are often seen as pertinent in healthcare as they encourage and encompass the collaboration of many actors, which was also seen during the pandemic.
- IPPPs that include private finance have been used extensively in the health sector, including in countries such as the UK, but with mixed results.
- Various countries are still experimenting with different forms of PPPs in healthcare and are focusing in entrepreneurship, SIBs, and improved management contract practices.

Key terms

- Bundling of services: When services and financial instruments are bundled together in contracts in PPPs.
- Public-private hybrids (PPHs): Roughly the same as partnerships.

DOI: 10.4324/9781003020844-3

Introduction

This chapter examines how partnerships continue to emerge in the health sector. Partnerships are almost natural in the health sector because partnerships enable very different organizations to work together on mutual challenges that cannot be solved by one organization alone. Partnerships were also important after the outbreak of the Covid-19 pandemic.

PPPs in the health sector bundles hospital infrastructure and clinical services (Ferreira and Marques 2021). The health sector has gone though many of the same changes in public governance and management that others sectors have, including governance paradigms such as the NPM and NPG and Digital Era Governance (Ferlie 2022). Ferlie also points out that the health sector in Europe has been prone to many private sector management impulses from management thinkers and consultants. This would include inputs from Harvard Business School professor Michael Porter and large consultancy firms like McKinsey (Ferlie 2022: 115).

The health sector in Europe, and the organization of a market for private sector providers, is also influenced by the European Union rules and initiatives (Martinsen and Vrangbæk 2008).

Much of the talk in health sector is about public-private hybrids (PPHs). PPH is a recent term, but it covers much the same territory as partnerships. Cappellaro, Compagni, and Dacin (2024: 247) characterizes PPH as:

> Public-private hybrids (PPHs), which combine public and private actors in collaborative arrangements of value forms, have emerged to provide solutions to complex social needs that traditional organizations have been unable to address. PPHs can generate societal value by producing innovations and services that would be otherwise lacking as well as gains in efficiency.

So it's close to the partnership definitions mentioned in Chapter 1.

Controversies in partnering for improved health

Torchia, Calabro, and Morner (2015) provide a systematic literature review on PPPs in the healthcare sector in peer-reviewed journals from 1990 to 2011. They found that six lines of research can be identified: effectiveness, benefits, public interest, country overview, efficiency, and partners. Although PPPs are used more in the health sector, the results regarding effectiveness and efficiency are still undecided and needs more research. Torchia and Calabro (2018) find that there is a need for increasing the governance standards of PPPs and they present evidence from Italy to support this argument.

Bishop and Waring (2016) see four areas of development with PPPs in healthcare. The first area was concerned with introducing private finance in infrastructure PPPs. A critique here is that these types of PPP projects were found to involve "inequitable sharing of risk, offering poor value for money and leaving public sector organizations with high levels of debt" (Bishop and Waring 2016: 463). A second area was concerned with public and private sector organizations to collaborate in earnest, despite the challenges. A third area is the emerging prominence of PPPs with a private sector/private finance profile that caused a decline in the delivery of public services and work conditions within the public sector. The fourth area is the ongoing debate about performance and outcome of PPPs which remains contested to many observers.

Waring, Currie and Bishop (2013) provide a contingent study of the use of PPPs in healthcare. They use empirical material from England in their work. Their approach is ethnographic. They adopt the idea that PPPs are organized in a "loose" or "tight" manner, citing Hodge and Greve (2005: 6). They point to four factors that shape the relationship in partnerships: (1) dependence on partners regarding finance, strategy, and resource sharing, (2) the strategic orientation of leaders, (3) the composition of the professional workforce, and (4) the management approach to service and workforce organization. The research therefore contributes to a contingent understanding of PPPs and how they are operationalized on the ground.

Santandrea, Bailey, and Giorgino (2016) examine the question of value for money in PPPs in the UK from a "fragility perspective". They offer a systematic literature review and content analysis. They identify several sources of uncertainty (fragility) which come from the financial structure, inadequate ring-fencing of risks and contractual inflexibility. They recommend a diversification of funding sources, more flexibility/adaptability in the contracts, and improved risk governance.

Ferreira and Marques (2021) discuss if PPPs outperform public hospitals regarding quality and access. Their empirical data are from studies in Portugal. PPP hospitals can deliver services just as good as public hospitals, their research shows. PPPs and public hospitals are on equal level.

Aydin and Altingdag (2023) examine the experience with PPPs in the healthcare sector in Türkiye. Türkiye is one of the OECD countries with most infrastructure PPPs in the hospital sector. Eighteen hospitals were built using the PPP approach. This study is therefore an important addition to the literature on partnerships in the health sector. The national PPP policy in Türkiye has been ongoing since 2013. The article examines the policy development in Türkiye for PPPs. The finding is that PPPs influenced the long-term financial viability of Türkiye by weakening it, and Türkiye's government had to abandon the PPP policy when constructing new hospitals. The PPP policy led to bottlenecks for practitioners: PPP contracts had to be cancelled in the end which can affect the taxpayers. Türkiye's prime PPP policy for hospitals is not the showcase example anymore.

Acerete, Stafford, and Stapleton (2011) report on the renowned "Alriza Model" in the Spanish healthcare system. Spanish banks were important in establishing the infrastructure PPP model in Spain in the healthcare sector.

Pereira, Ferreira, and Marques (2021) take a critical look at the experience with PPPs in healthcare in Portugal. Casady and Baxter (2022) examined how public procurement occurred through the use of PPPs during the Covid-19 pandemic.

Ways ahead for partnerships in healthcare

Greve et al. (2022) demonstrate how infrastructure PPPs can emerge in the hospital sector in Denmark even in the absence of a well-defined national PPP policy.

Kosycarz, Nowakowsa, and Mikolajczyk (2019) examine if the PPP model can be used for healthcare provision in Poland. They find that using PPPs can be an opportunity if the following items are taken into account: Changes to the contract with the payer for healthcare services, stable economic and legal conditions, appropriate allocation of risks, enough experience in both the public sector and the private sector, use of a competent and reliable private sector partner, and sufficient initial capital to get the project started.

Kociemska (2023) discusses how to seek public value from PPPs with a specific focus on SIBs. Kociemska uses a database on SIBs from around the world. SIBs can be away to reinvigorate PPPs according to these authors while others remain more sceptical about the potential of SIBs (Smyth and Stafford 2025).

Kareba et al. (2023) examine how managers handle contracts. They examine how information sharing is affected by contractual arrangements, using an empirical example from the healthcare sector.

Cappellaro, Compagni, and Dacin (2024) trace trajectories of value generation and capturing by PPPs and discuss levels of multi-level governance in healthcare. The article appears in the journal *Organization Studies*. They call them "Public-Private Hybrids" (PPHs). They identify three types of trajectories: (1) long-term value generation by stable partnerships, (2) long-term value generation by transient partnerships, and (3) interrupted value generation by terminated partnerships. They then relate these trajectories to the multi-level governance aspect. They point to field- and organizational-level governance compensatory mechanisms that, together, allow long-term value generation. They come up with the term "transient hybrids" as a distinct organizational form for long-term value generation.

Sinnisamal et al. (2016) discuss the view of entrepreneurs in social and healthcare service provision. The empirical material for the investigation is interviews with entrepreneurs in Finland. They find three main factors that are important in relations to entrepreneurs and partnerships: the nature of the partnership itself, business aspects, and tension builders. Collaboration between a local government and entrepreneurs will depend on mutual understanding and consensus.

The wholegrain partnership case

This section concerns the case of the Danish Wholegrain Partnership ("Fuldkornspartnerskabet"). The Guardian UK (2025) published an article about the Wholegrain Partnership documenting the development, entitled "The Wholegrain Revolution in Denmark: How Denmark Changed the Diet and Health of their Entire Nation" (23 April 2025). Rachel Dixon, the journalist writing the article, said: "If it possible to make a country healthier one slice of rye bread at a time? It's the rocketing wholegrain consumption of the Danes is anything to go by, absolutely".

The Wholegrain Partnership began with a challenge: People in Denmark were not eating enough healthy food. This was a concern from the Food Agency within the Ministry of Agriculture and the NGOs of the Danish Cancer Society and the Danish Heart Society. In some ways, this was a wicked problem that a healthy diet was deteriorating in Denmark. At the same time, there was a more pragmatic and business-like challenge: The bread and bakery industry faced a problem at the same time. The sale of bread was declining, and new diets focused on other food products than bread. This put the bread factories and companies, including bakers, in a situation where they had to do something to reverse the trend to stay in the market.

Organizations from three sectors: the public sector, the private sector (companies), and the civil society and NGO sector came together to confront the problem. Together they came up with the idea of making a campaign to make people eat more wholegrain products as a part of their daily food consumption. The idea of making wholegrain the centre of the campaign resonated with organizations from all three sectors.

Around the same time, the Food Agency within the Ministry of Agriculture was looking for new ways to create public awareness campaigns for a more healthy diet. The private sector companies, especially the large bread companies, were eager to innovation and develop new products so they could please consumers again and at the same time enable them to get a healthier diet. The NGOs of the Danish Cancer Society and the Danish Heart Society were also eager to try out new ways of campaigning for getting their health messages across in a new way.

Together these particular organizations plus a few more, including the large retailers with supermarkets, created a new partnership: The Wholegrain Partnership. The idea was to promote the intake of wholegrain in various products. A number of actions followed from this decision.

The first action was to establish a scientific knowledge base for how wholegrain improved a healthy living lifestyle. It would be impossible to make a mere marketing campaign and not have the basic facts ready. A report was commissioned from the Technical University of Denmark. This report provided the benchmark that the partnership later worked from. It was established that a daily intake of 75 g of wholegrain was recommended (later changed to

90 g). People in Denmark did not eat sufficient amounts of wholegrain per day so there was a challenge to be met. The second action was to establish a common label that would visually convey the message that was a product endorsed by the Wholegrain Partnership. The partnership came up with an orange logo that was put on products to demonstrate that the products had enough wholegrain in them. This later turned out to be a brilliant idea as the logo became easily recognizable. The third action was to make wholegrain an integrated part of the official Danish diet recommendations. The Food Agency was in charge of the official recommendations, and wholegrain was put on that list with a recommendation of 75 g per day.

There are 28 organizations that have joined the partnership (August 2025). These organizations ranged from very large, international bread and food companies like Nestlé and Schulstad to ordinary baker associations and smaller food companies. The big NGOs were present as mentioned: The Danish Cancer Society and the Danish Heart Association. The Danish Cancer Society hosted the secretariat of the partnership in the beginning, but the secretariat later moved on to Danish Industry, the large business association organizing most of Denmark's larger companies.

The question was how to organize this new partnership? It was agreed to make a formal organization with a board consisting of organizations from all three sectors. The board presented a strategy that the secretariat would work with. The strategy was conceived as a three-year strategy which would be up for renewal when the current one expired. The organizations in the partnership also agreed to pay a membership fee based on the size of the individual organizations. The partnership did not hire a CEO as such, but employed a Head of Secretariat. The board consisted of a Chair of the Board from a Danish food company and two vice-Chair of the board; a government manager and a person from an NGO (the Danish Heart Association). Other members were from Danish companies. The Confederation of Danish Industry had an observatory role.

The secretariat was rather small with only a few employees. The secretariat relied a lot on goodwill and in-kind appearances from people in campaigns. For example, several well-known sport stars agreed to appear in advertising as an in-kind gesture.

The way the partnership worked was to promote many activities to get the message across to people as customers and citizens that wholegrain should be an integrated part of their daily diet. The partnership also used the media a lot and arranged an annual "wholegrain day" with activities such as handing out breakfast to train travellers. The partnership also encouraged companies to innovate and to come up with new types of products with wholegrain in them. This challenge was accepted by some of the major companies, also international companies, which saw it as an opportunity to test new products on a stable market like the Danish market. More products came into the retail shops so consumers had more wholegrain products to choose from.

Rikke Iben Ness, the Head of the Secretariat, stated in 2025:

> In other countries, it may not be the norm that that you work together across government agencies, health NGO's and businesses. In Denmark, it feels quite natural, not least because of our strong culture for associations and our high degree of trust, and there's a great potential in that. That's why we are pleased to inspire other countries to "dare" to form partnerships.
>
> (Fuldkornspartnerskabet, homepage, August 2025)

The Wholegrain Partnership also kept track of awareness of the wholegrain logo. This figure has risen steadily throughout the years. The wholegrain logo is now recognized by 69% amount of Danish citizens in 2025, and out of these, 80% say the use it for inspiration when doing their shopping. There are 1,097 products in the marketplace carrying the logo (2019 numbers).

Making a public or shared value contribution has been the aim of the Wholegrain Partnership, and to some degree, the Wholegrain Partnership has succeeded in doing that. There are now many more wholegrain products in the retail supermarkets than when the Wholegrain Partnership began in 2008. More Danes than ever recognize the wholegrain logo. The intake of wholegrain products has gone up so Danes now eat 82 g of wholegrain per day. The coalition in the partnership has been maintained and there are 28 stakeholders in the partnership, including many well-known organizations and companies. The experience of the Wholegrain Partnership demonstrates what coming together on a single idea (of promoting wholegrain intake) can do for a partnership's value creation success.

Lessons from the Wholegrain Partnership case

What lessons can be drawn on how partnerships are organized from the Wholegrain Partnership case? Theoretically, the section will make use of the model that John Bryson and colleagues have been working on and have presented in various publications.

First, a clear goal is needed for the partnership to get going. In the Wholegrain Partnership, it was to improve the national health diet of the citizens and respond to a downturn in the market for bread products seen from the private sector side. It could be discussed how pressing these challenges are, but they were all challenges that several organizations felt the need to take up and to form a partnership around.

Second, an active management strategy is essential to keep the stakeholders in the partnerships engaged. Stakeholder-organizations join partnerships because they want to see them move forward and to create results and public- and shared value. Therefore, the partnership managers, often the head of secretariat, need to come up with activities that stakeholders can meet around, and which can help push the whole partnership forward.

In the Wholegrain Partnership case, the head of secretariat did not have much formal power as such, since that formal power rested with the boards, but they could take initiatives, like proposing to use sensors in new smart city solutions for parking spaces, organizing "the wholegrain annual day", and congregating stakeholders for meetings on "the open landscape". The head of secretariat has to be innovative and keep the stakeholders to the course of action all the time.

Structurally, the Wholegrain Partnership case had a three-year rolling strategy. The strategy was open to renewal at the end of the period, but there was also the possibility that the partnership would be dissolved if the public value had been achieved (this has not happened yet, though). Partnerships introduce a relatively clear governance structure which suggests a link between the board, the management (the heads of secretariats), and the people working on the actual mutual partnership activities on the ground. The Wholegrain Partnership was also data-driven to a certain extent. The Wholegrain Partnership worked strategically and consistently with collecting data about their performance. The Wholegrain Partnership used data systematically to track how many people recognized the orange wholegrain logo, how many wholegrain products were sold, and how much intake of wholegrain products people digested.

Fourth, the power relations need to be taken seriously in the partnerships. Even though the term partnership might envisage an organization where stakeholders share resources and risks, it is crucial to acknowledge that the different stakeholders enter with very different levels of resources. In the case of the Wholegrain Partnership, the bigger organizations probably had the most impact judging by their place on the board. But it was not only one sector that was the most powerful. Representative organizations from all three sectors were thought to be equally powerful.

The Food Agency within the Ministry of Agriculture had the authority of the state behind it and was the one organization who issued the official health recommendations. One of these recommendations involved the intake of wholegrain so in that respect all the organizations were dependent of the authority of the Food Agency. The big bread companies and the big retail chains, like COOP (Danish supermarket chain), were also represented on the board. These represented the "big business" and had the power resources of both producing and distributing the products of wholegrain to the customers. Without them, customers could not access products containing wholegrain. The NGOs represented many of the people who believed in healthy living, both from a nutrition point of view, but also from a personal health point of view. Two of the most powerful NGOs were the Danish Cancer Society and the Danish Heart Society who lend their resources and credibility to the partnership.

Fifth, the Wholegrain Partnership was able to exhibit results that could lead to public or shared value creation. The Wholegrain Partnership which aimed for more healthy eating habits and which succeeded to a certain extent in making Danes eating more wholegrain products and recognizing the wholegrain logo to use in their shopping routines.

Partnering in managing the pandemic

The story of how government officials tried to prepare for- and combat Covid-19 is a fascinating one and told by Michael Lewis (2021) in his book *The Premonition.* It is about how the central US health authorities really early focused on the pandemic and began to organize in partnerships. The idea was the US government alone could not solve all of the issues that were at stake, but had to rely on getting advice, knowledge, research and development, and production capacity from the private sector. The teams knew that not everyone was going to be successful in finding out how to deal with Covid-19, but they also knew if the one of the teams made it, or if an invention were to come out of it, it would be worth the effort. In fact, one of the key discoveries in combatting Covid-19 resulted from this process as one of the teams did become successful.

Governments all over the world have tried new ways of collaborating with the private sector in dealing with Covid-19. The Danish government initiated a committee designed to a national crisis management situation. This committee drafted persons from the private sector whom the government knew was good at managing difficult tasks. One of the tasks was to get enough protective equipment and to enter big contracts with companies from the private sector to buy enough protective gear. The private sector CEOs and other experts who were summoned to do the job, performed this to high satisfaction of the government. In a very short time of about a month, the Danish government had entered a sufficient amount of contracts for Covid-19 protective gear thanks to get the efficient collaborative structure the NOST committee provided.

One instance where the collaboration did not go so well was in a more traditional competitive contract situation in the Covid-19 battle in Denmark. The government wanted to have a new supplier of rapid Covid-19 tests. So, it put the contract to the market. The former supplier had just set up a whole logistics infrastructure and was performing well, but the regions had to follow EU procedures for competitive tendering. The contract was announced and several bids came in. One bid was from the original supplier. Another bid came from the organization SOS International and its sub-contractor. Their bid was 30% the price of the original bidder. SOS International and its sub-contractor won the contract. But it was a case of "winner's curse". SOS International and especially the sub-contractor did not have the logistics in place. Since this was an urgent and important task of rapid Covid-19 testing, the whole Danish test strategy was at stake. The sub-contractor did not have the logistics in place, and the workplaces were not up to hygiene standards expected. Within a week, the Danish regions involved cancelled the contract. The former supplier, Falck, was asked to take over the contract and reassume the task. This was an example where a competitive tendering process did not go as planned. The regions returned to a more partnership-oriented strategy by collaboration with Falck, which had been a trusted supplied of Covid-19 rapid tests recently.

A general way the Covid-19 crisis has been tackled has been to collaborate with pharmaceutical companies in developing vaccines against Covid-19. The company Moderna was already in April 2020 advocating for at PPP solution that involved the federal government in the United States together with private companies for developing an effective vaccine in an unprecedented short amount of time.

The process for these PPPs follows what Barbara Grey has characterized as three distinct phases: (1) problem-setting, (2) direction-setting, and (3) implementation. We would add the creation of public value in the tradition of Mark Moore of Harvard to the phase of "implementation".

The OECD has also been pointing to experiences with handling Covid-19 in its different member states. The OECD argues that collaboration is key to science, technology, and innovation efforts in the Covid-19 response. Collaboration in the future is encouraged along the principles of transdisciplinary research, new public-private funding mechanisms, and stronger collaborative models ("Revolving global challenges and crises through international collaboration", 12 January 2021).

A new architecture for a system of international co-operation that comprise existing institutional arrangements for country-focused development assistance, a new pillar focused on the provision of public goods ("Redesigning international co-operation finance for global resilience", 22 December 2020).

How can the multi level governance approach be used in the Covid-19 response? OECD has issued a publication on "The territorial impact of Covid-19: Managing the crisis across levels of government" (10 November 2020).

Covid-19 has taught everybody about pandemic preparedness (Dickinson, Yates and O'Flynn 2024). The role of development finance in helping development countries' health systems prepare and respond to outbreaks is examined here. Developing countries risk being exposed extraordinarily to future outbreaks ("Strengthening health systems during a pandemic: the role of development finance. In OECD Policy Response to Coronavirus (Covid-19)", 25 June 2020).

One paper argues that there has been too much focus on efficiency in the first wave of response to Covid-19. Instead, the focus should be on resilience ("A systemic resilience approach to dealing with Covid-19 and future shocks – in OECD policy response to Coronavirus (Covid-19)", 28 April 2020). One issue is how businesses have responded to Covid-19 and what their responsibilities are. OECD has discussed "Covid-19 and responsible business conduct" (16

April 2020). OECD has previously argued for "triangular co-operation" which is said to include sound national ecosystems to support triangular partnerships through high-level political will, guiding documents, institutional structures, partnerships, resources and management procedures ("Enabling effective triangular co-operation" OECD Development Policy Papers 23 December 2019). There seems to be widespread agreement that the Covid-19 response has triggered a new era of co-operation between public sector organizations and private sector organizations (both companies and NGOs). It is a question how they can collaborate even more in the future.

What were the issues still pending in the public-private collaboration for the Covid-19 response? One of the issues was that the collaboration was still bound up in contracts and contractual obligations. They do not yet seem to have entered a partnership type of arrangement. The contracts for vaccines are for specific types and numbers of vaccines. It is a transactional approach to a contract for the most part. Second, it did not seem that the governments had found a sufficient way to distinguish between large multi-national companies and smaller companies and NGOs. The case with the small Danish vendor that suddenly won a large contract shows that governments find it hard to make suitable due diligence arrangements when dealing with companies in the Covid-19 era. All companies apparently looked like the same to the Danish government in this specific case. Third, it does not seem as if there is a very clear management and leadership style.

Jacob Torfing and colleagues believed that the Covid-19 crisis triggered a need for a more robust governance system (Ansell, Sørensen and Torfing 2025). They identify the concept of "turbulence" as covering the extra difficulties governments around the world have found with dealing with Covid-19. They argue that the ordinary bureaucratic structures and the usual political leadership characteristics are sufficient in a situation like the Covid-19 situation. Instead, they advocate for a more decentralized and flexible system of governance that can show more robustness. Therefore, their argument is that the Covid-19 crisis was a form of game changer for the public sector and for public leadership. Covid-19 means that there is a need to collaborate with many more organizations outside the traditional bureaucracy.

The OECD has assembled a lot of material regarding country responses to Covid-19. Research from Norwegian scholars Christensen and Lægreid (2020) shows that countries like Norway found a way of balancing different demands. The Australian researcher O'Flynn (2021) explores in the same vein as Ansell, Sørensen and Torfing (2025) how the Covid-19 crisis can impact the field of public administration and the way that public organizations relate to each other and to private sector organizations as well.

What can we learn from the Covid-19 response so far about partnerships? The problem identification is relatively clear from the outset: There is a new virus and it is causing harm. The cure is to find a vaccine, which has now been found and tested by the end of 2020. The partnership structure in the first phase of finding a vaccine has been relatively loosely structured and had the characteristics of a portfolio management system where different clusters or partnerships were organized. In handling the crisis and distributing tests to the citizens, and securing preventive and protective tools, there has been an intense collaboration with private sector organizations. The formal structure of these partnerships is less certain, and many collaborations have rested on traditional competitive contracting schemes. Other times the contractual arrangements were suspended for a short while. In the implementation phase that will lead to public value creation in the sense of a return to normalcy, getting rid of the virus, and making a secure health environment for citizens, governments partnered with both companies and organizations to make sure the public value of a health environment is re-created. Here also, NGOs play a role in focusing on vulnerable citizens and creating programmes that will enable these citizens to engage with the rest of society again.

This means that we can divide the PPP approach to Covid-19 into different categories:

- Partnerships for procuring and securing personal protective equipment
- Partnerships for maintaining service delivery to citizens
- Partnerships with citizens through co-creation for complying with stricter regulations
- Partnerships for economic rescue packages and programmes to the private sector
- Partnerships for making Covid-19 tests and expanding test capacity
- Partnerships for developing a vaccine
- Partnerships for rolling out the vaccines

To some extent, they were very different approaches to involving the private sector. Procuring personnel protective equipment meant dealing with both existing companies and contractual agreements and also speed procurement with entering whole new contracts in a very short time horizon. Partnerships for delivering services to citizens meant that existing lines of delivery had to be kept up and others renewed. Partnerships on compliance with restrictions involved a public communication plan and a constant dialogue and information effort to keep citizens in the loop.

Partnerships for economic rescue packages and programmes to the private sector meant dialogue and negotiations with key organized business interests. In the Scandinavian countries, this meant tripartite negotiations between government, business, and labour. Many agreements have been made and rescue packages have been prepared and agreed upon. Partnerships for providing Covid-19 tests developed quickly as the need for more test capacity expanded. Governments had to enter contracts with private providers to keep up with the demand for more tests. Procurement procedures were followed, but as we have seen in the case of Denmark, some providers did not live up to the standard and suffered from what Simon Domberger (1998) once referred to as "the winner's curse" because they could provide the service and the infrastructure they had promised. There was emerging partnerships being built for test capacity, but it would take some time for the relational quality to be present. Partnerships for developing vaccines are probably the partnerships in the Covid-19 crisis that attracted the most attention. The US government used a sort of portfolio approach described in a *Time Magazine* article where several teams or clusters were working on different aspects of the vaccine programme or vaccine effort. Some of these efforts continued to become contracts and new partnerships while other efforts or clusters were discarded. Moderna called for a partnership approach early on in April 2021 and asked that the federal government step up its partnership ambitions in the search for a Covid-19 vaccine. Partnerships for rolling out the vaccine means that contracts have been signed with the pharma companies, and in the EU, the European Commission was the smart buyer in Kettl's (1993) terms on behalf of its membership countries. The roll-out of the vaccination programme requires a new infrastructure that also involve some of the private sector companies. All in all, there are various types of partnerships for the various kinds of tasks in the Covid-19 response.

Vrangbæk (2022) discusses the lessons and long-term implications of the Covid-19 response in Denmark for a resilience perspective. The article finds that while the first stage was characterized by flexibility and team spirit, the longer-term effects appear to be negative for nursing staff, including burnout and attrition. Although collaboration was seen early on between actors, and between levels of government, there are lessons to be learned for handling future crises.

Conclusions

This chapter has focused on the many varieties of partnering in the health sector. The health sector is one of the most complex sectors with many organizations from both the public sector and the private sector working together. The health sector has a long history of establishing and implementing partnerships. The Covid-19 crisis tested the partnership idea, and also demonstrated what partnerships can achieve.

Discussion questions

1 How did public-private partnerships make a difference in the period of Covid-19 and why?

2 What are the main characteristics of the health sector that makes it prone to PPPs?
3 In your opinion, are there limits to how many stakeholders can be included in a PPP in the health sector – and where is that limit then?

References

Acerete, Basilo; Anne Stafford & Pamela Stapleton. 2011. "Spanish Healthcare Public-Private Partnerships: The "Alriza Model"" *Critical Perspectives on Accounting* 22(6), 533–549.

Ansell, Christopher; Eva Sørensen & Jacob Torfing. 2025. *Robust Public Governance in a Turbulent Era: Theoretical Framework and Empirical Experiences*. Cheltenham: Edward Elgar.

Aydin, Yunus E. & Hallin Altingdag. 2023. "How Do Public-Private Partnerships Affect Public Service Principles? A Case of City Hospitals in Türkiye" *Public Works Management and Policy* 29(3), 496–508.

Bishop, Simon & Justin Waring. 2016. "Public-Private Partnerships in Health Care". In Ferlie, Ewan; Montgomery, Kathleen & Pedersen, Anne R. Eds. *The Oxford Handbook of Health Care Management*. Oxford: Oxford University Press, pp. 459–480.

Cappellaro, Gilua; Amelia Compagni & Tina M. Dacin. 2024. "Trajectories of Value Generation and Capturing by Public-Private Hybrids: Mechanisms of Multi-Level Governance in Healthcare" *Organization Studies* 45(2), 247–253.

Casady, Carter B. & David Baxter. 2022. "Procuring Healthcare Public-Private Partnerships (PPPs) Through Unsolicited Proposals During the COVID-19 Pandemic" *Journal of Public Procurement* 22(1), 6–16.

Christensen, Tom & Per Lægreid. 2020. "Balancing Government Capacity and Legitimacy: How the Norwegian Government Handled the Covid-19 Crisis as a High Performer" *Public Administration Review* 80(5), 774–779.

Dickinson, Helen; Sophie Yates & Jannie O'Flynn. Eds. 2024. *Research Handbook on Public Management and Covid-19*. Cheltenham: Edward Elgar.

Domberger, Simon. 1998. *The Contracting Organization*. Oxford: Oxford University Press.

Ferlie, Ewan. 2022. "Public Management in Health Care: With Examples from the English NHS" in Schedler, Kuno. Ed. 2022. *Elgar Encyclopedia on Public Management*. Cheltenham: Edward Elgar, pp. 112–115. https://doi.org/10.1016/j.seps.2020.100798

Ferreira, D. C. & R. C. Marques. 2021. "Public-Private Partnerships in Healthcare Services: Do They Outperform Public Hospitals Regarding Quality and Access? Evidence from Portugal" *Social-Economic Planning Sciences* 73. https://doi.org/10.1016/j.seps.2020.100798

Greve, Carsten; Lene Tolstrup Christensen; Christina D. Tvarnø, Sandie Nøhr & Sarah M. Denta. 2022. "Public-Private Partnerships in the Healthcare Sector: Limited Policy Guidelines, but Active Project Development in Denmark" *Journal of Economic Policy Reform* 25(2), 121–135.

Guardian, The. 2025. "The Wholegrain Revolution: How Denmark Changed the Diet and Health of Their Entire Nation" https://www.theguardian.com/lifeandstyle/2025/apr/23/the-wholegrain-revolution-how-denmark-changed-the-diet-and-health-of-their-entire-nation

Hodge, Graeme & Carsten Greve. eds. 2005. *The Challenge of Public-Private Partnerships*. Chelthenham: Edward Elgar

Kareba, Florence; Roehrich, Jens K.; Conway, Steve & Turner, Jack. 2023. "Information Sharing Public-Private Relationships: The Role of Boundary Objects in Contracts" *Public Management Review* 25(11), 2166–2190.

Kettl, Donald F. 1993. *Sharing Power. Public Governance and Private Markets*. Washington, DC: Brookings.

Kociemska, Hanna. 2023. "Accessing Social Value from Profit-Oriented Public-Private Partnership" *Journal of Entrepreneurship* 14(3), 370–389.

Kosycarz, Ewa A.; Beata A. Nowakowsa & Marcin M. Mikolajczyk. 2019. "Evaluating Opportunities for Successful Public-Private Partnership in the Healthcare Sector in Poland" *Journal of Public Health* 27(1), 1–9.

Lewis, Michael. 2021. *The Premonition. A Pandemic Story*. New York: W.W. Norton.

Martinsen, Dorte & Karsten Vrangbæk. 2008. "The Europeanization of Health Care Governance: Implementing the Market Initiatives of Europe" *Public Administration* 86(1), 169–184.

O'Flynn, Janine. 2021. "Confronting the Big Challenges of Our Time: Making a Difference During and After Covid-19" *Public Management Review* 23(7), 961–980.

Pereira, Miquel A.; Diego C. Ferreira & Rui C. Marques. 2021. "A Critical Look at the Portuguese Public-Private Partnerships in Healthcare" *The International Journal of Health Planning and Management* 36(2), 302–315.

Santandrea, Martina; Stephen Bailey & Marco Giorgino. 2016. Value for Money in UK Healthcare Public-Private Partnerships: A Fragility Perspective" *Public Policy and Administration* 31(3), 260–279.

Sinnisamal, Janne; Pekka Leviäkangas; Tommy Autio & Elina Hyrkäs. 2016. "Entrepreneurs' Perspectives on Public-Private Partnerships in Health Care and Social Services" *Journal of Health Organization and Management* 30(1), 174–191.

Smyth, Stewart & Anne Stafford. 2025. "The Privatisation of Finance: Can Private Finance Save the World?" in Hodge, Graeme; Greve, Carsten & Reeves, Eoin. Eds. *Research Handbook on Privatisation*. Cheltenham: Edward Elgar, pp. 246–266.

Torchia, Mariatheresa; Andrea Calabro & Michelle Morner. 2015. "Public-Private Partnerships in the Healthcare Sector: A Systematic Review of the Literature" *Public Management Review* 17(2), 236–261.

Torchia, Mariatheresa & Andrea Calabro. 2018. "Increasing the Governance Standards of Public-Private Partnerships in Healthcare. Evidence from Italy" *Public Organization Review* 18(1), 93–110.

Vrangbæk, Karsten. 2022. "Lessons and Long-Term Implications of the Covid-19 Response in Denmark from a Resilience Perspective" *European Journal of Public Health* 32(3), Supplement 1, 2 pages.

Waring, Justin; Graham Currie & Simon Bishop. 2013. "A Contingent Approach to the Organization and Management of Public-Private Partnerships: An Empirical Study of English Health Care" *Public Administration Review* 73(2), 313–326.

Wholegrain Partnerships (DK). website: www.fuldkorn.dk

Selected readings

Casady, Carter B. & David Baxter. 2022. "Procuring Healthcare Public-Private Partnerships (PPPs) Through Unsolicited Proposals During the COVID-19 Pandemic" *Journal of Public Procurement* 22(1), 6–16.

A piece that focuses on the role public-private partnerships played in healthcare during the pandemic. Both authors have a long experience with researching and advising on public-private partnerships in international contexts.

Ferlie, Ewan. 2022. "Public Management in Health Care: With Examples from the English NHS" in Schedler, Kuno. Ed. 2022. *Elgar Encyclopedia on Public Management*. Cheltenham: Edward Elgar, pp. 112–115.

This text provides a good overview of the main issues in healthcare management, and it has examples from the UK which was one of key countries to have experiences with public-private partnerships.

4 Partnerships for cities

Learning objectives

By the end of this chapter you should:

- Understand the trends towards smart cities
- Assess the ways in which tech companies, including Big Tech companies, invest and involve themselves in projects for smart cities and what challenges smart cities make for governments.
- Have developed knowledge on what it takes to be a partnership manager in relation to smart cities

Key points of this chapter

- Smart cities have evolved as a tempting way for cities to provide services for citizens.
- Partnerships between local governments and tech companies can be filled with challenges and involve attention to detail and contractual negotiations.
- Partnership managers need skills to deal with tech companies in smart city contracts and to be able to include citizens in developing and rolling out smart city solutions.

Key terms

- Smart city: "an umbrella concept used to describe the use of technology in cities to improve public services, to increase efficiency

DOI: 10.4324/9781003020844-4

(by reducing costs and resource consumption), to address societal challenges and to foster collaboration between citizens and government" (Sancino and Hudson 2020: 701).

- Digital Era Governance (DEG): The central role that digitalization plays in a wide-ranging series of alterations as to how public services are organized (Dunleavy & Margetts 2023: 186).

Introduction

This chapter examines how partnerships are used in cities to encourage urban development. The main challenge is to find out how partnerships can be of use in new initiatives in cities. Among key themes are the smart city, the climate-friendly city, and the inclusive city. Sometimes they are combined.

Smart city has been defined as "an umbrella concept used to describe the use of technology in cities to improve public services, to increase efficiency (by reducing costs and resource consumption), to address societal challenges and to foster collaboration between citizens and government" (Sancino and Hudson 2020: 701). To Geva and Siemiatycki (2025: 235), "Smart cities, broadly defined, aim to translate the opportunities of the digital age into concrete urban planning and governance tools". The smart city has received much interest and encouragement from business. The business side saw a new market develop before their eyes which they could develop for- and together with local governments. Smart cities have also been used as testing grounds for new technologies.

Another way of describing smart cities is:

> By definition, Smart Cities are those that integrate information communications technology across three or more function areas. More simply put, a Smart City is one that combines traditional infrastructure (roads, buildings and so on) with technology to enrich the lives of citizens.
>
> (Cisco CEO and Vice President in Green 2019: 3)

In writing about the smart city (called "datapolis" in his research), Meijer (2018) came up with these questions:

> How do choices for data-structures emerge from dominant perceptions, power alliances and (institutional rules? How are the perceptions, strategic interactions and rules for decision-making influenced by data-infrastructures? How do these interactions between institutional structures and technology result in the emergent properties of smart cities?

A review of the literature on smart cities and governance found that perspectives included (1) government of a smart city (focus on good governance), (2) smart decision-making (innovation in decision-making processes), (3) smart government administration (innovative ways of organizing), and (4) smart urban collaboration (innovative governance networks). Many articles had other focuses than the above-mentioned aspects (Meijer and Bolivar 2015). A recent review also found that smart governance in cities did not necessarily contribute to more sustainable cities, as the empirical evidence so far is mixed (Tomor et al. 2019).

Summarizing a public governance perspective on smart cities, Meijer noted that:

> The public governance perspective we developed stresses that the smart city should be understood as a complex set of interactions between private, public and civil society actors. They all have systems for collecting and processing data, and they also exchange and use data from other actors.
>
> (Meijer 2018: 203)

Controversies in partnering for smart cities

Not everyone is overtly thrilled with the prospect of smart cities. There are several ways to discuss this. One is to provide a cautious approach and talk about a "smart enough city" (Green 2019). Others see the advent of Big Tech into cities where partnerships are more transformative than you would first imagine. Siemiatycki provides a realistic look on how partnerships, Big Tech, and smart cities go together.

Green (2019: 10) proposed the concept of the "smart enough city" which he described as follows:

> It is a city where technology is embraced as powerful tool to address the needs of urban residents, in conjunction with other forms of innovation and social change, but is not valued for its own sake or viewed as a panacea. Rather than seeing the city as something to optimize, those who embrace the Smart Enough City place their policy goals at the forefront and, recognizing the complexity of people and institutions, think holistically about how to better meet their needs.

This seems like a more realistic conception of how a practical smart city approach can work out in local governments.

With this definition, Green points to a key part in the more critical literature on smart cities. Smart cities have been accepted as a concept, but critics do not see why it should be a carte blanche to Big Tech to almost take over cities with democratically elected governments. And the technology solutions that may look dazzling today, risk being outdated in a few years' time and what being "smart" look like then? Green's proposed concept of a smart-enough city nails this debate stream as cities can improve life for citizens using technology, but it suffices that cites are smart enough, not overly smart. Green's discussion of strategies in his hometown of Boston illustrates this point.

Siemiatycki (2022) argues that partnerships for urban developments are special and should not be treated as just a project like any other project. He writes:

> For urban scholars, a school is not a road is not a subway is not a hospital. PPPs are not evaluated narrowly as financial instruments or project management tools. Rather, each type of infrastructure, and in fact each project itself, is vastly different in its role and impact on the communities in which it is developed.
>
> (Siemiatycki 2022: 171)

Financial analysts and investors see PPPs as investment objects, some asset to yield a rate of return and not necessarily as a unique infrastructure project that may benefit a local community.

Siemiatycki points out the challenges ahead:

> The arrival of new players in the urban infrastructure space, particularly global investors tech firms, non-profits and philanthropists, has the potential to considerably reshape the political logics of urban PPPs. PPPs are seen as a part of a larger political ideology where financialization is restructuring the governance of cities.
>
> (Siemiatycki 2022: 171)

This way, there is a shift in the way cities are run, as Siemiatycki sees it. Big Tech companies have an interest in trying out their new technology in the world's leading cities. Big Tech companies and financial investors provide brand new services, and they also market the firms as the organizations of the future. The companies hope and bet on that their innovative solutions in one city will inspire the next city to adopt or buy their services. In that way, it is a competitive market and an increasingly global market for smart city services that are provided by private sector companies.

Siemiatycki sees partnerships as broader than just financial instruments and still wants to explore the collaborative opportunities in the PPP approach:

> A future research agenda is needed that both uncovers the flawed logics and negative outcomes of the current practice of PPPs, and also points to alternative ways of providing infrastructure that will achieve results that are more equitable, sustainable and just. While the PPP brand may be damaged, reinvigorating the place of meaningful partnerships and collaboration in city building is as important as ever to tackle the most pressing urban challenges.
>
> (Siemiatycki 2022: 172)

The "damaged PPP brand" that Siemiatycki here refers to is the often-heard criticism that partnerships with the private sector are seen as money-making facilities and not really partnering in the sense of the word where the actors involved have equal power and influence and share the same aspirations.

The critique here concerns how many researchers and investors treat partnerships. To some of them, a partnership is like an investment object. If it is procuring a new school building, a new part of a harbour, a new hospital, or a new part of a city, it is still an investment object. City planners and scholars of partnerships view it differently. Many partnership definitions focus on how public sector organizations and private sector organizations seek each other out to establish whether there are grounds for a closer collaboration on processes and products that have public value contribution perspectives. Seen from a purely financial matter, this approach is not really important, and that is what Siemiatycki and others oppose.

Nukpezah, Apalowo, and Abutabenjeh (2025) see the following elements influencing engagement with smart cities occur: multiple funding sources, collaborative governance, barriers to smart city technology (SCT), opportunities for adoption of technologies, local political institutions, and local socio-economic and cultural factors. Nukpezah et al. find that multiple sources of funding are important, that a PPP is a prerequisite for showing commitment to a smart city concept because it ties the private sector into the deal, and that horizontal collaboration also matters. The authors predict that "Cities with more literate and informed citizens who participate in government and seek more information from government are likely to be more successful using SCT (smart city technology)" (Nukpezah, Apalowo and Abutabenjeh 2025: 10).

Others refer to the new state of affairs in cities as a privatized city. Astrid Voorwinden (2021) examines "the privatized city: technology and public-private partnerships in the smart city". Voorwinden argues that the use of PPPs in smart cities challenge the ways that citizens and other actors can create public value. For-profit companies are highlighted and given advantages in smart cities. Providing legislation is not enough as these private companies take over more tasks and are not held accountable. Public norms need to be extended also to private companies who are active in developing smart cities.

The case of Sidewalk Labs, see more in the section "The case of Sidewalk Labs in Toronto", supports this viewpoint about attempts at making more privatized cities. Sidewalk Labs were given advantages in the partnership they made with Waterfront Toronto according to several researchers (Nelischer 2024; Filion, Moos and Sands 2023). Sidewalk Labs was heavily engaged in the planning process of the proposed city development. In the end, Sidewalk Labs withdrew from the project as the case description below has more on.

Cruz and Sarmento (2017) presents a sceptical view on infrastructure PPPs and their ability to change and adapt to the needs of smart cities in the future. Georgiou (2023) adopts some critical reflections on what it means to be humans in digitalized cities. Her recent book is a thorough investigation of what life is like as a digital citizen.

Cardullo and Kitchin (2019) are generally suspicious of PPPs and smart cities when they argue that there is a neo-liberal, market-based logic behind "citizen-focused smart cities" in Europe. They put forward an idea of an alternative conception of smart citizenship that is going to be needed. This confirms the tendency of a lot of researchers to apply critical lenses to smart cities. Specifically, researchers point to the overtly marked-based logic that Big Tech companies and other types of companies tend to have towards smart cities. Big Tech companies may view smart cities as business opportunities, almost like showrooms for new products that they are trying to sell to city governments all around the world.

Brenaugh, Hammerschmid, and Stockreiter (2025) reviewed the literature on 74 articles that investigated PPPs and digitalization projects, and they focused especially how the public values were part of the digitalization projects. The authors both examined the internal governance mechanisms and the broader effects in society. The public values that were found most present were efficiency, participation, and accountability. Second tier of public values were accessibility, trust, and proportionality. The authors also found that the public sector needed to safeguard the public values in the PPPs.

Ways forward for partnering for smart cities

Almarri and Boussabaine (2025) examine the critical success factors for PPPs in smart city infrastructure projects. They argue that PPPs are one of the most effective ways of countering budget constraints, but also that the success of PPPs will require massive investments to make them work.

The budget constraints are what traditionally have led governments to pursue the possibility of PPPs. Especially relevant in this context are IPPPs. Here, private finance means that new types of infrastructure can be provided. It functions as a way to create debt in an instance. Cities can finance a new infrastructure using private finance and "buy now", and then "pay later" as the payments on the credit card debt has to be delivered.

Quan and Solheim (2023) explore the research agenda on PPPs and smart cities. They identify four main themes that have emerged in recent years: localness, stakeholder complexity, tension, and trust-building. This confirms the complexity that increasingly surrounds city governments. A city government cannot go it alone anymore but has to partner with external stakeholders on a variety of policy issues. They have to build trust with private sector partners, but as partnership theory tells us, there is also management of risks involved.

Mu, Wu, and Haersdan (2023) examine how pre-contractual relationships can help develop PPPs for smart cities. They find that a formal contract is best aided by pre-contractual activities that use relational governance. They point out that a relational governance approach helps reduce substantive, evaluative, technological, and procedural uncertainties in a project. Their findings come from studying a case study of a PPP smart city project. This confirms a general point in the literature on contract. A contract is more than the formal, written contract itself. As Durkheim said, "not everything in a contract is contractual". The relationship between the partners and the trust building are extremely important for a contract to work. Also, what happens after a contract has been signed, in the implementation phase, is important. Hodge et al. (2018) found that the implementation of a contract is also dependent on the energy that partners put into it. Hodge et al. found that for infrastructure PPPs, the private sector partner had a habit of sending "the A team" for negotiations of the formal contract itself. When the contract was to be implemented, it was more "the B team" or "the C team" that was involved and this sometimes caused conflicts between the partners. Brown et al. have written extensively of the type of contracts that are necessary for a relationship to work. If is often helpful to distinguish between transactional contracts and relational contracts. As the names implies, transaction and a hard approach to contracts are features of the first type, while trust-building and continuing dialogue are some of the hallmarks of the second type of contracts.

Pianezzi, Mori, and Uddin (2023) discuss PPPs in smart cities in Japan and have found a curious case. The idea of partnership is deeply ingrained in Japanese culture and therefore it is important to learn about how PPPs in smart cities fare in Japan. The authors find that a more neo-liberal, market-based outcome is not necessarily on the cards, and that a more transactional approach is unhelpful. Japan prepares itself for the long haul and do not necessarily go for short-term wins in relation to smart cities and PPPs.

This research finding is interesting because the much of the PPP literature concerns cases from Europe, North America, Australia, and New Zealand. A case from Japan with a different administrative culture is therefore important. It illustrates the point made by Greve and Hodge (2013) that different cultures are important to take into account when examining PPPs. The virtue or necessity of partnership can be different if you come from a culture where are there strong divisions between the public sector and the private sector, and where many activities have been privatized, or if you come from a culture that has valued collaboration and seeking consensus. Japan is a country where partnership is a more natural part of society than, say, the United States or the UK with a strong competitive business culture. OECD (2021) has done a thorough study of how US cities use data innovatively in cities.

Secinaro et al. (2019) argues for a hybrid model when developing smart city projects from a planning perspective. This is hoping that the best features can be extracted from the public sector and the private sector. It focuses on what Donald Kettl (2006) has called the collaboration imperative.

Sancino and Hudson (2020) explores how leadership in, of and for smart cities have emerged in Europe, America, and Australia. It is done though a multi-case study research design. They see four modes of smart city leadership: smart cities as digital government, smart cities as digital driver for economic growth, smart cities as an open innovation platform, and smart cities as platform for digital economy. The smart-city-as-digital-government is akin to what researchers have been describing as Digital Era Governance (DEG), a public governance paradigm identified by Patrick Dunleavy and Helen Margetts (2023) (see also Torfing et al. 2019). This means that much of the government's service comes through digital services, and that a main interface between governments and citizens are through digital interfaces. Smart cities as digital drivers refer to the notion that new technologies are expected to drive both local economies and national economies. By partnering with tech companies, a local government can enhance its chances of being an attractive location for companies to invest in. That again means more jobs, and more jobs then mean bigger tax revenues for the local government. Smart cities as open innovation platforms refer to the surge; there has been within public organizations to embark on innovation journeys and to open innovation labs. It is a way of saying that governments can work smarter and better if they facilitate innovative processes and involve input from citizens to make improvements on their services. Many countries, including in Australia and New Zealand, have experimented with innovation labs. They have put people with different backgrounds and profiles together in innovation labs, and they have often build physical labs inside government departments. Smart cities as platforms for a digital economy concern the growing industry of digital companies that was alluded to above also. The companies that are attracted to an area can be more tech-based and can form clusters. Many cities strive towards this and also to be a home for these companies; although a lot of different variables go into making these industrial districts, it is not an easy task.

Hofstad et al. (2022) compare the governance strategies of Copenhagen and Oslo as they strive to work collaboratively in addressing climate change.

Bauer, AbouAssi, and Johnston (2022) argue that collaboration is affected by institutional characteristics as well as personal characteristics of the leaders. The empirical basis is a study of local governments and non-profit organizations in Lebanon. This is a relevant perspective as it also focuses on leaders in addition to the institutional features that surround smart cities.

Example of a partnership strategy from a development organization in Copenhagen is By og Havn (City and Harbour). By og Havn says that it will:

- Contribute to new initiatives and methods in sustainability within construction industry and the property market
- Work in partnerships to enhance CO_2 reducing solutions
- Actively participate in partnerships with companies and organizations who support the mission from the Paris Agreement
- Work in partnerships with utilities to invent new energy and utility solutions in Nordhavn

- Work in partnerships with the transport sector as many lorries/trucks are involved in city development
- Actively participate in partnerships on culture, sports, and associations in the harbour area, for example by renting out space in limited periods (see By og Havn forretningsstrategi 2024–2027)

The case of Sidewalk Labs in Toronto

The case of Sidewalk Labs in Toronto is a remarkable story. The city of Toronto wanted to develop a new area of the harbour. They were eager to turn into a smart city innovation site. The city government wanted to be prolific and signal that Toronto was in the forefront of adopting new technologies. The area in the harbour was called "Quayside". The city government did not have capacity to develop the site on its own. Instead, the city government envisioned a PPP. To find a partnership in the private sector that could help the government development Quayside. The same time, Sidewalks Lab, a Google-owned company were interested in smart city development and actively looking for a space to develop its vision. A PPP was soon set up between the city government and Sidewalk Labs. It was accompanied by a grand vision of making the city a technologically advanced place and platform.

Nelischer (2023) focused on evaluating the PPP of Sidewalks Labs in Toronto, Canada. Nelischer analysed a smart city project at the quayside in Toronto, interviewed 35 people, and made participant observations and doing document studies. Nelischer found that there was reduced government insight and accountability, conflict of interests abounds, and the private sector was given more advantages and had influence. PPPs pose risks to the public planning process. We go more into the case as follows.

Filion, Moos, and Sands (2023) go into depth on the failed "Sidewalks Lab" in Toronto, Canada. There were three reasons for the abandonment according to the authors: opposition movements towards surveillance, the fragmentation of the neoliberal block, and the failure on strategy by Sidewalks Lab itself.

In the negotiations, it seems that Sidewalk Labs had the upper hand. Research has pointed out that the contract was influenced to a large degree by Sidewalk Labs' wishes. The city government was eager to develop the Quayside area and therefore did not want to put a lot of restrictions on Sidewalk Labs. The expertise of building a smart city lay with Sidewalk Labs. Sidewalk Labs was therefore involved in a considerable way in the planning of the smart city project and had more insights and knowledge into the project than the city government's own planning staff.

At first, there were high hopes for the Sidewalk Labs project. The city government would lead the way in the world of smart cities. Google and Sidewalk Labs would get a testing ground that could be used as a showcase to other city governments. Citizens would benefit from advanced services. But soon things started to take a different turn. City government planners complained that the Sidewalk Labs people were too dominating and they did not always respect or understand the public administration context they were working in. Getting permissions and gathering support can often take time in a public administration, and Sidewalk Labs did not always seem to acknowledge that. In true private sector innovation spirit, Sidewalk Labs did not have the patience to wait for what for them was cumbersome government bureaucracy. Local protest groups started to appear. They were highly critical of the whole project. Especially, the future surveillance was a big issue with the protesters. Sidewalk Labs would build a city full of sensors and technologically advanced items that citizens feared compromised their personal space.

Sidewalks Labs upped the ante once the plans were underway. Instead of the agreed part of Quayside, Sidewalk Labs argued that it should have more space to build on. Sidewalk Labs proposed to take control of an even larger site next to Quayside, and thus planning to expand the smart city to an even larger geographical area. This move caused further protests among the citizens, and the city government was also taken aback a little. Sidewalk Labs argued that a larger area could encompass an even greater vision for the smart city they were constructing.

The controversies became bigger as protests continued to get better organized, and Sidewalk Labs vision challenged the capacity of the city government. Then, abruptly in 2020, Sidewalk Labs announced that it was pulling out of the project altogether. The reason cited was instability in the property market and the uncertainty of what lay ahead with the advent of Covid-19. Also the city government was taken by surprise. In the media in Toronto, there was speculation about other reasons. One was a change of strategy in the Google company itself. Sidewalk Labs was folded into the Google company again and stopped being a separate company. Others speculated that Sidewalk Labs had underestimated what it was like to deal with a city government over such a complex planning issue.

Researchers who have examined the Sidewalk Labs case note the following. The partnership was not an even partnership, and the partnership format itself gave Sidewalk Labs as a private company some advantages over the city government. Sidewalk Labs had the necessary expertise, and the city government conceded too many planning decisions to Sidewalk Labs. Nelischer (2024: 269) points out that "The challenges created by the co-creation partnership were intensified by the vast resource and power asymmetry between Waterfront Toronto and Sidewalks Lab". Filion, Moos, and Sands (2023) lean towards the same point when they point to three obstacles to the Sidewalk Labs project. The first is the opposition coming from citizens' protests that focused on fears of surveillance. Second, politically, there were conflicting strategies with one line of the politics, the liberal one, preferred long-term economic strategies for partnering with the private sector, and another line of politics – a conservative one – that did not approve of any subsidizing of projects like Sidewalk Labs. Third, the focused approach of Sidewalk Labs that disregarded the public administration context, and that Sidewalk Labs were not transparent in its aims. Did it only want to land, or did it actually want to build a new kind of PPP?

Citizens' concern over surveillance was not given adequate attention in the partnership, as the partnership was focused on the smart city idea and vision. There was little accessible way for citizens to let their worries be heard other than through more loud protests.

What are some of the lessons learned for managing partnerships? Safeguard the contract and make sure that partners have a basic mutual understanding of what is at stake. Set out a common vision and stick with it, and do not change it the way Sidewalk Labs did relatively soon into the project period. Have a mechanism or dialogue process where mutual problems can be addressed. It did not seem that there was one in the Sidewalk Labs project as Sidewalk Labs suddenly ended the contract without any prior notice or warning. It also points to the backing of the organizations entering the partnership. Sidewalk Labs had the support of Google in the beginning, but then suddenly Google's company strategy changed and then Sidewalk Labs strategy also change. The city government had a strategy from the beginning of wanting to develop a harbour area into a smart city district in Toronto, but had apparently forgotten to get the full support from the citizens of Toronto, as the protests witnessed.

Discussion: Challenges for partnering for cities

What are the prospects for the smart city when viewed through the lenses of the analytical framework of this book? The policy state implies that politicians are eager to suggest introducing smart city measures. This would be compatible with politicians seeking technological solutions to problems. The drive towards more technological initiatives is also examined in Dunleavy and Margett's concept of DEG. The DEG as a public governance paradigm will fit well with the more technologically optimistic view on data use that is a part of the smart city movement. The collaborative self, the concept from Helen Sullivan (2022), suggests that organizations are open to partnerships, and that they want to be part of common endeavours. The smart city is a concept that want organizations to reach out to other organizations to address grand societal challenges – how to cope with advanced technological possibilities if you are a city trying to meet the demands of your inhabitants? Public managers within partnerships for smart cities have to be boundary spanners and bridgebuilders to be able to reach out to tech companies and to citizen associations and NGOs. This will acquire a lot of skills to negotiate with international tech companies, including the Big Tech companies, to secure a smart, and also a fair, deal when signing contracts for new smart city systems. The boundary spanning is one thing when increasing the area of influence, another thing is the actual bridgebuilding and coordination of different interests. This can be very tricky as tech companies press for smart solutions, but those solutions can lock-in the technological choices and create barriers for other companies' future solutions. Citizens may not even like being subjected to technological trial activities, and the protection of personal freedom also plays a bigger role now than it did when the so-called smart solutions were first introduced. The collaborative architecture consists of the arena which is the contractual relationship between a local government and the tech companies in question, the rules of the game which are also partly made up by the contract, and the actors which consists of local government managers and smart city managers, and sometimes citizens or NGO representatives. Further, the public value that is produced consists of more flexible and easier solutions in terms of technology to use for citizens and for local governments. In that respect, one can wonder if the specific smart city solutions produced by specific tech companies actually make a difference, or if citizens and cities can simply benefit from the broad technological development which does not require particular investments from individual local governments. Maybe local governments could just follow the technological developments and acquire off-the-shelf solutions for their citizens rather than enter contractual negotiations about developing new technological tools. In that way, local governments would take less risks on behalf of their citizens. This leads to the question of whom the partnerships are for? Are the partnerships for the citizens or the tech companies and their shareholders? Many of the critical voices in the literature cited above believe that the balance may be tipping towards the tech companies who benefit financially from the movement towards smart cities.

There is a link between the overall demands from the policy state – find smart solutions and use the technological advances developed by mainly the Big Tech companies and the concrete choices about how to produce public value that especially local governments find themselves in when they are faced with the challenge of making the life easier and smoother for their citizens with the aid of technology. Many times in that chain, things can potentially go wrong, or at least in another direction than intended. The combined effects across cities in a country mean that many different types of so-called smart city solutions can be arrived at, and consequently many different types of partnerships for many different forms of public value. The smart city vision was a decade ago; the big idea and partnerships in cities would support that vision, but now there are more empirical evidence coming out now of how cities implement smart city tools, devices and concepts. Some of the original enthusiasm has waned again and given space for more afterthought. The more remarkable cases, like the one with Sidewalks Lab in Toronto, also tell cautionary tales. It would also seem that some of the smart city technologies are now the same found in many cities and countries around the world. One thinks of the "Big Belly" wastebin that a particular company in the UK made and had marketing around, and many cities have now adopted that or similar tools. Another is the solutions for parking where several of the parking apps are international, or only seldom local anymore. These so-called smart solutions are in this respect just technologies or services linked to specific companies, and the innovation is taken care of by the companies themselves, and not through any elaborate local dialogue process with citizens.

Conclusions

The smart city phenomenon acquired a lot attention when it first came out. Together with new technological possibilities, and the expansion of cities, the smart city concept promised better and easier life for citizens, and the promise of fast city development. Smart cities were designed to make the promises of the digital age benefit city planning, as Geva and Siemiatycki (2025, 235) remarked. It coincided with a period where the governance and management of cities were getting more traction, and where public organizations and private sector organizations began to move closer to each other in newly formed partnerships. The PPP gave the collaboration a format that both public and private sector organizations could use.

A number of factors halted the speedy implementation of smart city projects. First, the Big Tech companies tended to become dominant in the project they engage in. They have the resources, the know-how, and also the expertise with smart city technology. Often, city governments cannot match the resource level that Big Tech arrives with. This points to power asymmetries pointed out theoretically by Bryson et al. (2015) and confirmed in empirical studies such as Nelischer (2024) and Filion et al. (2023). Second, the debate on surveillance capitalism has occurred, and smart city technology is seen by many citizens has enhancing the surveillance that is going on. This has led to a counterargument that we only need a smart-enough city as suggested by Ben Green, instead of the full-blown version of a smart city with all the censors and smart gadgets. Third, there is a fear among some observers and researchers that the smart city is an embodiment of a neo-liberal discourse and practice that have the effects of turning citizens into consumers and limiting democratic procedures and transparent work habits. There are many instances where smart city practice seems to strengthen the commodity side of a city and less so the community side of a city.

Discussion questions

1 What are the key ingredients needed for a city to be a smart city?
2 How and why are partnerships suited to the implementation of smart cities?
3 What are the key attributes that managers in partnerships need to have when they engage in smart cities?
4 What role do citizens play in smart cities, and do you think it is possible to include them more in smart city planning?

References

Almarri, Khalid & Halim Boussabaine. 2025. "Critical Success Factors for Public-Private Partnerships in Smart City Infrastructure Projects" *Construction Innovation* 25(2), 224–247.

Bauer, Zachary; Khaldroun AbouAssi & Jocelyn Johnston. 2022. "Cross-sector Collaboration Formality: The Effects of Institutions and Organizational Leaders" *Public Management Review* 24(2), 159–181.

Brenaugh, Jessica; Gerhard Hammerschmid & Simona Stockreiter. 2025. "The Prevalence of Public Values in Public Private Partnerships for Government Digitalisation: A Systematic Review of the Literature" *Government Information Quarterly* https://doi.org/10.1016/j.giq.2025.102048

Bryson, John; Barbara Crosby; Melissa Stone. 2015. "Designing and Implementing Cross-Sector Collaborations: Needed and Challenging" Public Administration Review 75(5), 647–663.

Cardullo, Paolo & Bob Kitchin. 2019. "Smart Urbanism and Smart Citizenship: The Neoliberal Logic of "Citizen-Focused Smart Cities" in Europe" *Environment and Planning C* 37(5), 813–830.

Cruz, Carlos O. & Joaquim M. Sarmento. 2017. "Reforming Traditional PPP Models to Cope with the Challenges of Smart Cities" *Competition and Regulation in Network Industries* 18(1–2), 94–114.

Dunleavy, Patrick & Helen Margetts. 2023. "Data Science, Artificial Intelligence, and the Third Wave of Digital Era Governance" *Public Policy & Administration* 40(2), 185–2014.

Filion, Pierre; Markus Moos & Gary Sands. 2023. "Urban Neoliberalism, Smart City and Big Tech: The Aborted Sidewalk Labs Toronto Experiment" *Journal of Urban Affairs* vol. ahead of print, 1–19.

Georgiou, Myria. 2023. *Being Humans in Digital Cities*. Bristol: Polity Press.

Geva, Yinnon & Matti Siemiatycki. 2025. "The Privatisation of Urban Planning: Smarter Cities?" in Hodge, Graeme; Greve, Carsten & Reeves, Eoin. Eds. *Research Handbook on Privatisation*. Cheltenham: Edward Elgar, pp. 229–244.

Green, Ben. 2019. *The Smart Enough City. Putting Technology in Its Place to Reclaim Our Urban Future*. Cambridge: MIT Press.

Greve, Carsten & Graeme Hodge. Eds. 2013. *Rethinking Public-Private Partnerships*. London: Routledge.

Hodge, Graeme A.; Colin Duffield; Emille. Bousson & Carsten Greve. 2018. "After the Ribbon-Cutting. Governing Public-Private Partnerships in the Medium to Long Term" *Australian Journal of Public Administration* 76(3), 330–351.

Hofstad, Hege; Eva Sørensen; Jacob Torfing & Trond Vedeln. 2022. "Designing and Leading Collaborative Urban Climate Governance: Comparative Experiences from Copenhagen and Oslo" *Environmental Policy and Governance* 32(3), 203–216.

Kettl, Donald F. 2006. "Managing Boundaries in American Administration: The Collaboration Imperative. *Public Administration Review* 66(s1), 10–19.

Meijer, Albert & Manuel P. R. Bolivar. 2015. "Governing the Smart City. A Review of the Literature on Smart Urban Governance" *International Review of Administrative Sciences* 82(2), 392–408.

Meijer, Albert. 2018. "Datapolis: A Public Governance Perspective on "Smart Cities"" *Perspectives on Public Management and Governance* 1(3), 195–206.

Mu, Rui; Peiyi Wu & Maidina Haersdan. 2023. "Pre-contractual Relational Governance for Public-Private Partnerships: How can Ex-ante Relational Governance Help Formal Contracting in Smart City Outsourcing Projects?" *International Review of Administrative Sciences* 89(1), 112–128.

Nelischer, Kate. 2024. Evaluating Collaborative Public-Private Partnerships: The Case of Toronto's Smart City Project" *Journal of the American Planning Association* 90(2), 261–273.

Nukpezah, Julius A.; Jubilee T. Apalowo & Sawsan Abutabenjeh. 2025. "Why Do Cities Go Smart? Investigating the Determinants of Local Engagement with Smart Cities Technologies" *Cities*. https://doi.org/10.1016/j.cities.2025.106036

OECD. 2021. *Innovation and Data Use in Cities*. Paris: OECD.

Pianezzi, Daniela; Yuji Mori & Shaddaz Uddin. 2023. "Public-Private Partnership in a Smart City. A Curious Case in Japan" *International Review of Administrative Sciences* 89(3), 632–647.

Quan, Xiangyu & Marte C. W. Solheim. 2023. "Public-Private Partnerships in Smart Cities: A Critical Survey and a Research Agenda" *City, Culture and Society* 32. https://doi.org/10.1016/j.ccs.2022.100491

Sancino, Alessandro & Lorraine Hudson. 2020. "Leadership in, of and for Smart Cities – Case Studies from Europe, America and Australia" *Public Management Review* 22(5), 701–725.

Secinaro, Silvia; Valerio Brescia; Davide Calandra & Paolo Biancone. 2019. "Towards a Hybrid Model for the Management of Smart *City* Initiatives" CITIES 116. https://doi.org/10.1016/j.cities.2021.103278

Siemiatycki, Matti. 2022. "New Frontiers in Planning" in Hodge, Graeme & Greve, Carsten. Eds. *A Research Agenda for Public-Private Partnerships and the Governance of Infrastructure*. Cheltenham: Edward Elgar, pp. 161–175.

Sullivan, Helen. 2022. Collaboration and Public Policy. London: PalgraveMacMillan.

Tomor, Zuzanna, Albert Meijer; Ank Michels & Stan Geertman. 2019. "Smart Governance for Sustainable Cities. Findings from a Systematic Literature Review" *Journal of Urban Technology* 26(4), 3–27.

Torfing, Jacob; Lotte Bøgh Andersen, Carsten Greve & Kurt Klaudi Klausen. 2019. Public Governance Paradigms. Competing and Co-existing. Chelthenham: Edward Elgar.

Voorwinden, Astrid. 2021. "The Privatised City: Technology and Public-Private Partnerships in the Smart City" *Law, Innovation and Technology* 13(2), 439–463.

Selected readings

Green, Ben. 2019. *The Smart Enough City. Putting Technology in its Place to Reclaim Our Urban Future*. Cambridge: MIT Press.

This is a well-written and accessible book by a former employee in Boston local government who has worked with introducing smart city measures in the city, but that have since reflected upon the proper use. His title indicates that we should maybe be more cautious about smart cities, and consider settling for smart enough.

Nelischer, Kate. 2024. Evaluating Collaborative Public-Private Partnerships: The Case of Toronto's Smart City Project" *Journal of the American Planning Association* 90(2), 261–273.

Here you can read more about the spectacular case of Alphabet's "Sidewalk Labs"-project at the harbour side in Toronto, Canada. The case is also referred to in the chapter, and here you can read the whole story about the development of the project and how high expectations was followed by more subtle assessments and in the end closure of the project. The case can help you understand some of the driving forces behind smart cities.

Siemiatycki, Matti. 2022. "New Frontiers in Planning" in Hodge, Graeme & Greve, Carsten. Eds. *A Research Agenda for Public-Private Partnerships and the Governance of Infrastructure*. Cheltenham: Edward Elgar, pp. 161–175.

Siemiatycki provides a thorough and convincing overview on urban planning today and shows what happens when initial big aspirations for partnerships meet the realities of financial investors and more specific planning challenges. The chapter sheds some much-needed realism into the debate on what partnerships can do for city planning.

5 Partnerships for the climate

Learning objectives

By the end of this chapter you should:

- Get a sense of how widespread partnerships have been used for addressing climate change
- Be able to know what empirical evidence there is for how partnerships work in climate issues
- Draw lessons from cases that describe processes of establishing partnerships for the climate

Key points of this chapter

- Partnerships are highly relevant for addressing climate change as it brings together many different organizations around a common goal.
- Some partnerships for climate change use the IPPP model that encourages use of private finance. However, it is often challenging to make the business case work.
- Partnership for climate change is hard work and there is mixed evidence of how well they work.

Key terms

- Sustainability issues in partnerships: This both deals with focusing on the environment and for creating suitable conditions for working in partnerships (i.e. is the organizational form sustainable in itself).

DOI: 10.4324/9781003020844-5

Introduction

Partnerships are present in relation to climate change. The UN sustainability goals set the global targets for what should be achieved with the climate. The Paris Agreement followed soon after in 2015, which committed all the countries that signed up for it to a determined course towards rescuing the climate. Goal number 17 in the Sustainable Development Goals reads "Partnerships for all the goals".

In the European Green Deal, the goal is to be climate neutral for the EU by 2050. The European Green Deal will make Europe climate neutral by 2050 boosting the economy through green technology, creating sustainable industry and transport, and cutting pollution. The EU sees itself as a global leader that establishes green alliances, setting global standards for sustainable growth, making climate issues part of international relations. The funding comes both from public and private finance. A European Climate Law means "to transform promises into legal obligations". The European Green Deal promises a Climate Pact that will make use of public consultation to bring together regions, local communities, civil society, businesses, and schools. The EU Climate Pact is an EU-wide initiative inviting people, communities, and organizations to share information, debate and act on the climate crisis, and to be part of an ever-growing climate movement. The EU Climate Pact is presented as being "an open, inclusive and evolving initiative for climate action". The EU wants to refurbish and renovate buildings:

> A refurbished and improved building stock in the EU will help pave the way for a decarbonized and clean energy system, as the building sector is one of the largest energy consumers in Europe and is responsible for more than one third of EU's emissions.

The EU has "a biodiversity strategy" that will put Europe's biodiversity on the path to recovery by 2030 for the benefit of the people, climate, and the planet.

C40 is an influential organization consisting of, initially, 40 great cities around the world, but now include many more as well as affiliated organizations. C40 reckons that 1,700 companies globally in the We Mean Business-coalition are recognizing that the transition to zero emissions is the way to secure a stable and viable economy in the future: "C40 works to connect cities with the private sector and drive innovation, maximizing the opportunity of joint climate action around the world".

The initiatives include: (1) City-Business Climate Alliance, (2) City Solutions Platform, (3) New Economies and Innovation Forum, and (4) Reinventing Cities. (More information on these initiatives can be found here: https://www.c40.org/what-we-do/influencing-the-global-agenda/engaging-the-private-sector/.)

All these initiatives bear witness to the fact that cities are deeply involved in the climate agenda and are taking steps to focus on concrete climate proposals and projects.

Controversies in partnering for climate change

Partnership seems like the obvious organizational form for addressing the issue of climate change because of the chance of getting several organizations to work collaboratively over a prolonged period of time towards a common goal. But there some issues that are not necessarily easy to handle in partnerships, and perhaps the expectations to partnerships are often too high? Partnerships are both singled out for maybe being able to facilitate new types of collaborations, but the time horizon of partnerships often leaves participants disappointed as quick results cannot always be achieved.

De La Cruz et al. (2022) discuss how the transition to cleaner energy solutions and sustainable development require better collaboration in PPPs. The article wants to explore hybrid PPPs for policymakers so they can use them in climate policies and institutional frameworks. This focuses on how partnerships can play a new and intermediate role the area of climate policy and sustainable development. This is important because partnerships can find a new role here.

Jensen and Dowlatabadi (2018) discuss how the public sector has turned towards including private finance in aspirations to finance low-carbon initiatives in a school district. The empirical case comes from Vancouver in British Columbia. Governments are sceptical towards creating debt for themselves, so they turn to private finance solutions which may hold the investment off the balance sheet. Private finance this way is, however, not a viable solution in the long run because if will still affect future generations, and governments should therefore recognize the need for proper investment levels up front instead of hiding behind a PPP scheme.

The discussion about hiding behind a PPP scheme is an ongoing discussion in the IPPP literature. One thing is to get finance for a particular project, it is quite another thing to actually have to pay for it. It is also about the type of risk-taking partners are about to take. There has been a huge stream of research devoted to the topic of private finance and risk sharing. Morris and Little (2018) address the crucial issue of climate change and infrastructure – the coming challenge.

Hancock, Ralph, and Ali (2018) write about a scheme in Bolivia where that country's hunt for lithium is enacted through the use of private finance and PPPs with foreign corporations.

This confirms the trend of IPPPs in whole new areas. The quest for lithium is on the agenda in geopolitics. IPPPs are also used by many companies and countries seeking advantages geopolitically. IPPPs became very popular in countries in Asia, including in China. They are therefore part of a trend of going into new areas.

Hessevik (2022) examines a PPP project called "The Green Shipping Programme" that affect the road towards low- and zero-emission shipping. The article describes the case of the Norwegian Centre of Expertise Maritime CleanTech cluster. Resources of individual network members that participate in the PPP can be mixed and matched, therefore extending the governance capacity. The types of expertise that can be combined include technical expertise, lobbying expertise, and relational capital.

This is a case where a PPP functions as a governance mechanism that can get many different partners with stakes in a project on the same page and work together within a common framework. The PPP is here seen as vehicle for collaboration where different kinds of expertise are brought together.

Hueskes, Verhoest, and Block (2017) discuss how sustainability considerations are built into infrastructure PPPs. The empirical material comes from 25 Flemish projects and cases. The authors find that sustainability considerations had played a relatively minor role in infrastructure PPPs, and that this was caused by the inability to formulate workable measures. Enforceable performance indicators are needed going forward if sustainability should be considered in these infrastructure projects.

This is in one part a significant finding that there may be talk on sustainability, but that in reality they mean very little in PPPs. In another interpretation, it might be a signal that it was too early for this type of sustainability issues to be built into PPPs.

Spraul and Thaler (2020) explore sustainability issues in PPPs. Their empirical material comes from the German public bathing and swimming pool sector. They point to both external factors such as regulation and industry self-regulation and internal elements including structure and processes of the partnership itself. They see it as a starting point for exploring sustainability and PPPs further.

Prinz, Roudyani, and Thaler (2018) strive to present an overview of the topic of sustainability and PPPs and make suggestions for a new research agenda. They conclude that "little empirical evidence confirms whether PPPs are appropriate instruments for accomplishing sustainability-related objectives". The research avenues they suggest are the following: (1) investigate sustainability as a core concept in PPP research, (2) develop or adapt measurement tools to capture different sustainability dimensions in PPP research, (3) apply rigorous success factor research to detect (combinations of) success factors that are relevant to the accomplishment of sustainability-related objectives in PPPs, and (4) build on sustainability management literature to elaborate on the success factors crucial for the actual achievement of sustainability-related objectives in PPPs.

Ansell, Sørensen, and Torfing (2022) explore the potential of local governments' contribution to the United Nations' Sustainable Development Goals. They put emphasis on co-creation and a strategy for partnerships.

Endo, Edelenbos, and Gianoli (2022) write about sustainable infrastructure. The authors have conducted a systematic literature review. PPPs and multilateral development banks play pivotal roles. Various horizontal governance modes are combined with various vertical governance structures. Striving for a sustainable infrastructure is goal number 9 in the Sustainable

Development Goals. "Green" infrastructure has been defined as: "a hybrid network of natural, semi-naturel, and engineered features within, around and beyond urban areas at all scales, which is planned and managed to provide multiple ecosystem services and benefits". In the literature review, IPPPs are the preferred model mentioned in 41 articles out of 85 articles. The definition used here is that PPPs are long-term co-operation between the public and sectors for infrastructure (and its) service provision by sharing roles and responsibilities, risks, costs and profits. Private finance plays an important role in filling the gap from missing public finance investment.

Meyer and Yusuf (2022) discuss the structuring of PPPs and the relationship to public value. The empirical material concerns the transport sector and more specifically transport projects in Virginia, USA. The authors review contractual documents. The study comes up with insights into how roles, relationships, and interactions of both public and private partners are incorporated into agreements to pursue public value. The public value part is using Mark Moore's concepts. The authors mention that research into the relationship between PPPs and public value is limited, and point to the few studies that exist, including studies by Tony Bovaird, and then highlight five types of public value: accountability, transparency, responsiveness, responsibility, and quality. They also find that the contract itself is essential: "A well-negotiated contract can provide benefits to both public and private sectors while offering potential solutions to some of the country's most pressing infrastructure problems" (see the "Conclusions" section).

Vecchi, Tanese, and Osborne (2022) ask: "Do public-private partnerships still have a future?". They argue for a new approach to PPPs that include Environment Social and Governance (ESG)/ Sustainable Development Goals (SDG) and the impact investment agenda, thereby contributing to addressing wicked problems. They therefore argue for a renewed approach to PPPs.

An active strategy to pursue public value through collaboration for the sustainable development goals was analysed by Van Gestel, Ferlie, and Grotenberg (2023).

The case of the P4G partnership

This is a case of a particular climate partnership. It is an international partnership, P4G, which is nowadays a Washington, DC-based organization that fights for the climate and for green growth (www.p4gpartnerships.org).

The background is the following: The country of Denmark hosted the COP 15 meeting in 2009. This was supposed to be a breakthrough meeting in the making of a new climate deal. The previous COP meetings had prepared the way. Now was the time to finally replace the Kyoto agreement and present the world with a new global climate deal. Unfortunately, the COP 15 meeting ended in failure. Only smaller agreements were made. Barack Obama explained in his biography about the COP 15 meeting. He writes that the UN general secretary had worked hard for Obama to attend the meeting even though Obama was sceptical about what could realistically be achieved. When the meeting began, China played a hard game, and the US–China competition on climate issues also influenced the meeting. In Obama's view, the COP 15 was almost doomed to fail from the beginning because it was very difficult to reconcile the views of the United States and China at the time. Obama writes that the Danish prime minister residing over the COP 15 meeting was put in an impossible situation. The US–China conflicts over climate were not going to be solved at the COP 15 meeting. Obama acknowledges that COP 15 in Copenhagen was merely a step along the way. The way, as we know now, first reached its peak in 2015 with the Paris Agreement.

The Danish government had pinned high hopes on an agreement in Copenhagen. There was a campaign for "Open Copenhagen" which was going to promote Copenhagen and Danish industry as open for the green growth business and the prospective of advocating for climate-friendly solutions on a broad scale. Danish industry had prepared a number of new products and innovations that were to be marketed under this banner. The Danish government had also prepared its national climate policy based on a successful outcome of the summit.

When the deal fell through, and COP15 was deemed more or a less as a disaster, the question was how to pick up the pieces? So much energy and manpower had been invested in promoting a Danish national green strategy that it seemed futile just to give up. The ideas came about in the government to try and form a partnership of a "coalition of the willing". Were some of the countries that were interested in pursuing a green growth agenda also interested in carrying on the conversation in a new partnership? So, one type of push came from the Danish industry. Another type of push came from the Ministry of Foreign affairs. They were looking for an additional way to conduct Danish diplomacy and to help save the reputation of Denmark – and to promote Danish business interests.

The choice by the Danish government was to make a partnership – a Global Green Growth Forum (3GF). The first meeting was held in October 2011 and opened by the Danish Prime Minister Helle Thorning-Schmidt and the UN General Secretary Ban-Ki Moon. The first two member countries of the partnership were South Korea and Mexico. Another batch of countries joined from 2012: China, Kenya, and Qatar. Ethiopia joined the partnership in 2014. These were the original member countries of the partnership.

First, the partnership was about focusing on concrete green growth solutions. The impetus was for the different business partners to find each other and to team up for specific projects and ideas they wanted to pursue. A number of concrete proposal within water management, battling food waste, etc. were established.

A governance structure of the partnership was also created. There was a board with representatives of the membership countries. The secretariat was run by the Danish Ministry of Finance, and was effectively in charge of managing the partnership. To help the secretariat getting a partnership up and running, the secretariat was relying on help and assistance from a number of consultancy companies and bureaus specializing in the way partnerships worked. These bureaus were issuing guidelines for partnerships and toolboxes that partnerships could use so the partners could benefit most from their membership.

The process of the working of the partnership was built around an annual wheel, which culminated in the annual conference in October where all the heads of states (or their representatives) got together in Copenhagen for a summit meeting. The UN general secretary was also known to attend. A preparation meeting was usually scheduled for the Spring where the programme for the October conference would be laid out in detail, and where all the necessary steps for creating a great annual conference were taken.

With the aid of consultants and with input from member countries and companies in those countries, several tools for creating successful partnerships were created. These included: "The 3GF Partnership Approach", which detailed how companies implemented partnerships in practice, and "the 3GF Value Chain Approach" detailing how companies were able to create value in these partnerships through several steps.

One of the issues in the 3GF partnership was the question of power relations. Obviously, the member countries were of very different size and capability. There were clear differences between how China approached partnerships to the way Ethiopia focused on partnerships. China has vast resources and know-how intended to make partnerships work while Ethiopia is a fragile state with many tensions and difficulties, which makes thinking about partnerships a lot harder to implement in practice.

Nevertheless, all of the member countries were committed to the partnership idea. Danish Prime Minister in 2016, Lars Løkke Rasmussen, was quoted at the annual meeting in 2016 as saying: "We do not achieve success if we do not work together. PPPs have demonstrated their value. They will contribute so the UN can reach its goals for a sustainable development".

The period for the 3GF partnership expired. The UN had agreed on the Sustainable Development Goals, and the world had changed. A new goal for the partnership was going to be formulated. The Danish government faced the choice of shutting the partnership down, or continue the partnership in a new format. The Danish government chose the latter option. A new round of negotiations was undertaken. The Danish government wanted to inspire the new partnership, but not necessarily lead it. The partnership was going embrace more stakeholders in the management of the partnership.

P4G was the name of the new partnership. It stands for Partnership for Green Growth and the Global Goals 2030. The member countries are Chile, Columbia, Denmark, Mexico, Vietnam, South Korea, Ethiopia, Kenya, and the Netherlands. A number of companies and associations have joined the

P4G partnership: Grundfos, the Kenya Private Sector Alliance, Novozymes, Vietnam Chamber of Commerce, the Global Green Growth Institute, World Resources Institute, World Economic Forum, and the C40 network of cities. The practical day-to-day management is taken care of by the World Resources Institute in Washington, DC. It says that the World Resource Institute "acts as the hosting partner for the P4G Global Hub", Global Green Growth Institute has the task of knowledge gathering for the partnership.

The P4G partnership today works on a number of issues and projects. P4G presents itself as "an innovation hub for partnerships". The partnership also describes itself as a "global network of do'ers". The focus areas in the SDGs are: zero hunger, clean water and sanitation, affordable and clean energy, sustainable cities and communities, and responsible consumption and production. Examples of partnerships include: a clean energy investment accelerator, Indonesia food loss and waste partnership, the zero-admission bus rapid-deployment accelerator, and the partnership for blended finance and water. P4G currently funds more than 30 partnerships.

The initial funding for P4G came from the Danish government who committed USD 33 million for the Partnership Fund and operational support. The Dutch government pledged USD 5.7 million.

The governance structure is that P4G is governed by a board of directors. The board consists of government ministers from the member countries, CEOs, and other leaders from institutions committed to pursuing sustainable development. Each P4G is country partner is engaged at the government level, and also have a national platform in those countries.

P4G states that:

> P4G partnerships include civil society, private and public-sector organizations who are working together to advance innovative and commercially viable project(s) in at least one of these five SDG sectors: food and agriculture (SDG 2), clean water (SDG6), clean energy (SDG7), sustainable cities (SDG11), and circular economy (SDG12).

The partnerships have to target green growth initiatives in developing countries.

P4G has developed "a P4G way" in five stages: Partnership development, co-funding, partnership acceleration, access to global P4G network, and commercial commitments. It is described the following way:

> The P4G way is our innovative partnership model that attracts private sector engagement and investment as co-partners with public and civil society sectors to work on start-up and scale-up projects for climate action and the SDGs. This model revolves around innovation with purpose, hyper-collaboration based on trust and acceleration. When organizations

> and countries agree on purpose, they can move past the short-term self-interest, to more lasting progress.

A P4G start-up can receive up to USD 100,000 in funding. A P4G scale-up partnership can receive USD 1 million in funding. The inaugural P4G summit was held in Copenhagen in 2018. A P4G summit was held in Vietnam in 2025.

Conclusions

This chapter has focused on partnerships for addressing the environment and climate change. The chapter has shown that partnerships are widespread in the climate change area, but that partnerships also face many challenges. There is often a lot of hope and aspirations pinned to partnerships in the climate change area, and the chapter documents how partnerships cannot always live up to the hype and that it is often too early to tell whether a partnership solution has worked or not because partnerships take time to evolve.

Discussion questions

1 How can the definitions presented in Chapter 1 be applied to the topic of sustainability and climate change?
2 Is there a need for new types of partnerships for sustainability or can the five types of partnerships from Chapter 1 be applied to this theme also?
3 What role does knowledge and scientific evidence play in managing partnerships addressing climate change?

References

Ansell, Christopher; Eva Sørensen & Jacob Torfing. 2022. *Co-Creation for Sustainability: The UN Sustainable Development Goals and the Power of Local Partnerships*. Bingley: Emerald Publishing.

De La Cruz, Pinilla; Andrea Giovanna; Rodrigo Rabetino & Jussi Kantola. 2022. "Unveiling the Shades of Partnerships for the Energy Transition and Sustainable Development: Connecting Public-Private Partnerships and Emerging Hybrid Schemes" *Sustainable Development* 30(5), 1370–1386.

Endo, Kei; Jurian Edelenbos & Albert Gianoli. 2022. "Sustainable Infrastructure: A Systematic Literature Review on Finance Arrangements and Governance Modes" *Public Works, Management & Policy* 28(4), 443–475.

Hancock, L.; N. Ralph; S. H. Ali. 2018. "Bolivia's Lithium Frontier: Can Public-Private Partnerships Deliver a Minerals Boom for Sustainable Development?" *Journal of Cleaner Production* 178, 551–560. https://doi.org/10.1016/j.jclepro.2017.12.264

Hessevik, Agnete. 2022. "Network-Led Advocacy for a Green Shipping Transformation: A Case Study of Governance Networks in the Norwegian Maritime Sector" *Regulation and Governance* 16(4), 1101–1118.

Hueskes, Marlies; Koen Verhoest & Thomas Block. 2017. "Governing Public-Private Partnerships for Sustainability: An Analysis of Procurement and Governance Practices of Infrastructure Projects" *International Journal of Project Management* 35(6), 1184–1195.

Jensen, Thor & Hadi Dowlatabadi. 2018. "Challenges in Financing Public Sector Low-Carbon Initiatives: Lessons from Private Finance for a School District in British Columbia, Canada" *Climate Policy* 18(7), 878–888.

Meyer, Martin & Juita-Elena (Wie) Yusuf. 2022. "Structuring Public-Private Partnerships for Public Value: Analysis of Two Transport Infrastructure Case Studies" *Public Works Management & Policy* 27(3), 295–314.

Morris, John & Richard Little. 2018. "Symposium Issue: Climate Change and Infrastructure – The Coming Challenge" *Public Works Management & Policy* 24(1), 3–5.

Prinz, Alexander; Nahid Roudyani & Julia Thaler. 2018. "Public-Private Partnerships as Instruments to Achieve Sustainability-Related Objectives: The State of the Art and a Research Agenda" *Public Management Review* 20(2), 1–22.

Spraul, Katarina & Julia Thaler. 2020. "Partnering for Good? An Analysis of How to Achieve Sustainability-Related Outcomes in Public-Private Partnerships" *Business Research* 13(2), 485–511.

Van Gestel, Nicolette; Ewan Ferlie & Sanne Grotenberg. 2023. "A Public Value Strategy for Sustainable Development Goals: Transforming an Existing Organization" *British Journal of Management* 35, 839–853.

Vecchi, Veronica; Angelo Tanese & Stephen Osborne. 2022. "Do Public-Private Partnerships still have a Future?" *Public Works, Management & Policy* 27(4), 335–336.

Selected readings

Hueskes, Marlies; Koen Verhoest & Thomas Block. 2017. "Governing Public-Private Partnerships for Sustainability: An Analysis of Procurement and Governance Practices of Infrastructure Projects" *International Journal of Project Management* 35(6), 1184–1195.

These public management scholars report from a research project in the Netherlands and Belgium and examine many of the main issues that infrastructure public-private partnerships deal with when they engage in sustainability and green transition projects.

Endo, Kei; Jurian Edelenbos & Albert Gianoli. 2022. "Sustainable Infrastructure: A Systematic Literature Review on Finance Arrangements and Governance Modes" *Public Works, Management & Policy* 28(4), 443–475.

Read more here on how financial arrangements in infrastructure public-private partnerships and accompanying governance modes influence the way sustainable infrastructure can be achieved.

Vecchi, Veronica; Angelo Tanese & Stephen Osborne. 2022. "Do Public-Private Partnerships still have a Future?" *Public Works, Management & Policy* 27(4), 335–336.

Short, but thought-provoking piece that sums up what the research on infrastructure public-private partnerships have achieved and then goes on to question the role of partnerships in the future to see if partnerships can adapt and be relevant for the age of sustainability and green transition.

6 A case for partnerships

Learning objectives

By the end of this chapter you should:

- Get a sense of how a case for partnerships can be made in today's complex world
- Understand how partnerships can contribute to the creation of public and shared value
- Get insights into some of the democratic concerns and dilemmas in using partnerships

Key points of the chapter

- A case for partnerships can be made because they are necessary components in today's complex governance architecture.
- Partnerships fulfil an important role as governments in what has been called "the policy state", constantly seek to engage in solutions to societal problems without having the organizational capacity inside the state to address those problems.
- To be sure, there will always be democratic concerns about using partnerships, but partnerships should be seen more as supplementary to democratic government rather than a replacement.

DOI: 10.4324/9781003020844-6

Key terms

- Public value creation which follows the Mark Moore understanding of exploring what public value can be created in collaboration among different types of organizations.
- Partnership managers are both boundary spanners, and, more to the point, nowadays bridgebuilders –the term used by Eggers and Kettl (2023) that act in the context of wicked problems and the policy state where solutions to complex issues must be addressed.

Introduction

This chapter focuses on how partnerships can remain a good idea and approach. Partnerships have been around for some time now, and there is evidence that they work well sometimes, and that they sometimes fail or do not go as planned.

The knowledge assembled shows a growing interest in partnerships and still more labels in close proximity to partnerships, including collaborative governance, hybridity, and networks.

Having absorbed all of these developments and changes, it would be fair to say, that there seems to be broad agreement about the following linage of arguments although the specific labelling may be different from writer to writer.

There are enough wicked problems and grand challenges in the world today to make it clear that organizations often want to work more closely together with other organizations and actors. Some of these challenges seem to get bigger and bigger, the climate crisis being the obvious example.

Governments are active in the policy state in seeking and offering policy solutions to what citizens need or require. More policy may mean more privatization, but more policy also means more partnerships. The more the areas governments choose to engage with, the more appetite there is for partnerships.

Actors form different kinds of PPPs to meet these challenges and find innovative solution to the problems that they face. They come in many shapes and forms. Some involve the use of private finance. Some involve the close collaboration with for-profit private companies, including private finance. And yet they share some of the key characteristics that are mentioned in the different definitions and that makes the hybrid form stand out.

Donald Kettl (2006) has called this drive for the "the collaboration imperative". It is necessary, and also increasing aspirational to work in partnerships.

Actors find themselves to be more inclined or interested in seeking collaboration. Helen Sullivan has coined the term "the collaborative self". By this, Sullivan means that actors will have a collective set of actions in them that they can draw upon.

Managing and leading PPPs is a task that demands many different roles and skills. Eggers and Kettl (2023) name the leaders as "bridgebuilders". Bryson compares leading partnerships to being a task that resembles "leading social movements" increasingly. One leader cannot do it all. The collective leadership is being mentioned more.

To understand the change in the overall system, Page and Stone (2023) talk about "a collaborative architecture".

On a formula it would look like this:

Wicked problems/grand challenges/the policy state → the collaboration imperative → the partnership → the collaborative self → the bridgebuilder → collective leadership → in a collaborative architecture.

Let us try to elaborate on these elements.

The wicked problem scenario is a well-known one by now. Nearly all partnership texts will start with this premise. Grand challenges and wicked problems are making it difficult to management of single organizations, therefore collaboration is needed. While the wicked problems are undoubtedly getting bigger (and more wicked at the same time), there is another dynamics that is also pushing the change. The policy state argument by Orren and Skowronek is that governments and politicians like to formulate and decide on policies. They cannot stop themselves. If they see a new subject area or public problem coming up, governments and politicians are inclined to suggest a new policy. In earlier times, citizens and politicians were vary of government influence and some even sought a "night watchman state" or a "minimal state". However, now there are so many problems and issues that politicians feel compelled to address in order to respond to citizens' demands, and the way they respond is by making a new policy. Think about internet regulation, environmental protection, or climate change initiatives and you get the picture. Here's the catch: Governments and politicians may want to make new policy, and also to create public value, but they do not necessarily want public sector organizations to run them. Here, they need partnerships instead. Governments are increasingly seeking partnerships to carry out all the promises that they have made when they make new policies in new areas.

It should be clear by now that managing PPPs does not take place in a vacuum. The premise is that there is an incentive to collaborate – we've established that with identifying the wicked problems and more recently the concept of the policy state. This context that makes PPPs necessary in our society is not likely to go away. Indeed, the concept of the policy state suggests that politicians will keep on responding to challenges by making new policies because they know that citizens and voters expect it of them. The answer here can be inspired by the strategic public management approach than suggests that change is ongoing. There's no stopping politicians anytime soon, and there are plenty of issues in society to address, so there will be a continuing need to manage strategically and to create and maintain partnerships. There is an incentive to collaborate – the collaboration imperative – and it means that managers must direct their attention to collaboration opportunities and possibilities. Running the day-to-day operations of the organization is all fine and have to be attended to, but at the same there is a need to reach out to other organizations for collaboration.

A formal partnership organization is one way of institutionalizing the collaboration. As noted many times, formal partnerships come in many shapes and sizes. We mentioned the most typical of them in the opening chapter, and through the thematic chapter, we have looked at partnerships in the healthcare sector, partnerships in cities, and partnerships concerning climate change. The elements (see the collaborative architecture section later on) on goal, arena, membership and mechanisms can "open up the black box" of the partnership organization as it were. Organizations need to be flexible and embrace "organizational ambidexterity – be it structural-spatial, temporal or contextual" (Page et al. 2021).

The collaborative self – a phrase coined by Helen Sullivan (2022) – describes the situation where the actors in the partnerships know that they have to work collaboratively. Not all of their actions are going to be about collaboration, but many of them of are, and that's the key point here. The collaborative self resolves some of tensions with how to work collaboratively that has dogged the literature for years. Are actors selfish or self-interested, and is the collaborative approach just a sign of altruism that does not hold in the long run? With the collaborative self, Sullivan argues that there are collaborative tools in actors that can be mobilized, and that is the important part when studying and analysing partnerships.

The bridgebuilders are those public managers that take on the task on managing the partnerships. They have been named many times – as brokers, as boundary spanners – and bridgebuilders seem as an apt and appropriate way to sum up their roles. Eggers and Kettl have discussed them at length in their recent book. The bridgebuilders are very important actors in managing PPPs. They can extend their work – and co-exist – with the broader managerial efforts by many actors in- and around a partnership. The concept of collective leadership has appeared to characterize this part of the management role in partnerships. Bridgebuilders are part of the collective leadership that takes place in and around partnerships. Collective leadership points to "an emergent theoretical umbrella that captures diverse scholarship on the shared, distributed, pooled, and relational aspects of leadership, its emergence and relationship to hierarchical leadership, as well as its impact on work and performance" (Ospina et al. 2020: 442). As Rosabeth Moss Kanter has put it, "Think outside the building for the future of leadership".

It is certainly a contrast to the all-encompassing strategic leader in the New Public Management-era or the stereotypical hands-on private sector leader. Managing and leading PPPs is different.

In a related article, Kettl (2006: 17) put it succinctly around 20 years ago:

> Devising new strategies to bring public administration in sync with the multinational, multisector operating realities of today's government requires a collaborative, network-based approach. That network-based approach, however, conflicts fundamentally with the symbol-driven imperatives of the way American politics approaches public administration.

This could be said about just any nation and not just the United States. The symbolic features of government with a prime minister or president, and one or more elected chambers, stand out clearly in citizens' minds and is enshrined in constitutions and founding documents. This is not the case with partnerships, networks, and hybrids, which do not have these symbolic features (except perhaps the image of the dispersed internet?).

The collaborative architecture is a concept that tries to show how the different elements making managing PPPs fit together. The collaborative architecture combines the institutional features with the organizational and processual features. Here, the collaborate architecture encompasses the previous elements in our formula mentioned above. Specifically, the collaborative architecture points to four elements: Goals, arenas, membership, and mechanisms (Page & Stone 2023: 19), as follows:

- **Open ended goals**: "The overall purpose of the collaboration, problems it formed, and solutions to those problems. Includes shared strategies, programs or projects to pursue collaborative purpose as well as statements about solutions to problems or ways to achieve collaborative goal(s). Goals are likely to have the properties of evolvability and specificity".
- **Interactive arenas**: "Arenas structures for designed for joint decision-making, deliberation or other interactions (e.g. sharing knowledge, expertise, or data relevant to the collective work). Arenas feature explicit rules for the roles, responsibilities and decision authorities of those structures".
- **Membership rules and norms**: "Explicit rules and behavioural norms that determine the boundaries of the collaboration. This component reflects the extent to which membership in the collaboration is open and accessible and different partners can engage in joint deliberations, decisions and strategies".
- **Mechanisms**: "Mechanisms includes processes and protocols as well as infrastructures that organize, leverage, and distribute knowledge, expertise, skills, and resources among collaborative actors".

As an example, consider the collaborative architecture surrounding the Wholegrain Partnership in Denmark. There were open-ended goals to get people to a more healthy diet by using wholegrain products. There were an arena that was the Wholegrain Partnership, including a governance structure that included a formal board. There were clear membership rules, including behavioural norms at meetings and rules for becoming a member. There were processes, protocols, and an infrastructure that distributed knowledge about wholegrain product developments and diet habits among citizens.

The concept of a collaborative architecture is related to the debate on systemic change that also Bryson, Crosby and Patton (2021) is focusing on. A recent definition of systemic change in the light of partnerships are: "the result of actions that lead to a significant alteration within a system, potentially leading to substantial impacts" (Clarke and Crane 2018: 308). Designing change interventions in complex systems requires skill and effort (van Tulder and Keen 2018).

When the policy state makes partnerships more necessary, then what are the drivers between the different partnerships models? IPPPs are promoted by governments, but also requested by the private sector. PPPPs are driven by government with the active participation of private sector companies and NGOs. Once a government solution or public intervention is proposed, there is a link to possible partners in the private sector in sight. PPIP are nudged on private sector companies and also by think tanks and NGOs who want to push ahead with innovation. PPSPs are driven forward by government and private sector companies in unison. Governments spot a new need among citizens, and private sector companies stand ready with prototype solutions (think electric cars). DPPPs are driven by international organizations and in close co-operation and contact with both private sector companies and NGOs.

What are the kinds of organizations most open to the partnership idea? If we take our inspiration from the Alford and Head table on wicked problems, but use it on the policy state instead, a 2 × 2 table could look something like this: One axis is about more policy issues or options versus less policy issues or options. The other axis could be on degree of organizational openness: high network-like way of organizing versus less network-like way of organizing, i.e. hierarchical. The square with most likelihood of partnership is the high policy issue, high network structure. The square with the less likelihood of partnership is the less policy issue, more hierarchical one. It could be argued that the trend in organizations is the more volatile, i.e. more policy issues, more network-like structure. It would also suggest that newer areas with more policy options available would be more suitable for partnerships (Table 6.1).

Table 6.1 Policy issues and way of organizing in partnerships

	Open systems approach to organizing	*Hierarchical organizing*
Many policy issues/ options	Partnerships: high probability	Still focusing on hierarchy: risk of overload of government
Few policy issues/ options	Partnership aspirations, but no real need for partnerships	Conventional stable hierarchy

Partnering for public value

How can partnerships help create public value? To examine this question, we must go back and look more close at Mark Moore's (1995, 2013) original conceptualization of public value and then follow what has happened since with the concept.

First phase

Mark Moore of the Kennedy School at Harvard developed the notion of public value when he studied, and learned from, the public managers who took executive education courses at Harvard. Moore found that these public managers did the best they could in the conditions they worked under. The public managers actually strived to make a difference – to create public value in the expression used by Moore. At the time, back in the1990s, the literature on public administration mostly saw public managers as bureaucrats in the Weberian sense of being efficient, rule-following civil servants. The growing literature on public management was focused on the manager as a can-do manager in the NPM. NPM famously had two strands: management techniques from the private sector and market-based governance. The American scholar Donald Kettl put it succinctly at the time: Letting managers manage and making managers manage. Managers had to be "free to manage" and pick up as many techniques from companies as they could. Or they were made to manage through the incentives in market forces that would put their organizations out of competition if they did not pursue more self-interested strategies. Moore discovered a third route that was an alternative to both bureaucracy and NPM. Through his empirical observations of public managers in action, Moore saw that public managers worked under political condition and in a context where rules were not always clear or clearly formulated. Public managers lived with much uncertainty, but they all had the citizens' well-being and the obligation to create value for the public as their guiding light. Moore thought of how private sector managers created private value for their shareholders, and using this analogy, Moore conceived of public managers as also creating value, albeit not for shareholders, but for the taxpayers and thereby the public. In this respect, the public manager was somebody who acted within the famous strategic triangle of seeking legitimization and support in the authorizing environment, using resources in the operational capacity, and thereby creating public value. But the focus in this initial concept was very much on the individual public manager. This was not so strange since the persons trained at the programmes in the Kennedy School were public managers. So that was the natural focus in a way.

Second phase

Moore started to acknowledge and work with the notion that public managers collaborated more with other managers in both the public sector and the private sector. Moore also noted that citizens and NGOs could be involved more in the creation of public value. This came forth in the book *Recognizing Public Value*. Moore also presented a public value scorecard that in more detail could help assess if public value had been created or not by public managers and organizations. At this point in time, a number of researchers began to elaborate and expand on Moore's initial ideas about public value creation. Janine Flynn was one of the first to see public value management as a sort of governance paradigm that could be understood as different from bureaucracy and NPM. The public manager here was now somebody who could reach out to other organizations in order to create and recognize public value. The empirical studies and the more theoretical elaborations that followed from a number of researchers, including John Bryson, Barbara Crosby, and their colleagues, focused on this aspect. The idea of public value creation were also embraced by scholars working with networks and the governance paradigm on NPG). Here, the public manager was seen as somebody who was either directing either a network of managers or organizations, or a manager who was part of a network and a governance structure. The centrality that Moore had allocated to the active public manager was now not necessarily taken for granted, but had to be empirically tested. Not so surprisingly, network researchers tend to focus on networks as their primary object of study, and less so about the individual public managers. Researchers in the network tradition began to argue that it was the network that created and produced public value. The public manager's role could be important, but it could just as well be some of the other organizations' managers who was going to be interesting to study. Through a number of forceful and convincing empirical analyses, this broader concept of how public value was produced through networks began to emerge. The literature on public value management began to be integrated in the network studies and also the literature on collaborative governance mentioned in Chapter 1.

Third phase

The concept of networks creating public value, and managers playing a role in that, was turned a notch upwards in theoretical ambition again when researchers began to argue for more systematic approaches to addressing grand societal challenges. The discussion on public value created in the first phase and second phase could very well be local, or regional in scope, but now in the third phase, researchers started to examine how systematic efforts involving many managers and organizations at a national level or international level could help address grand societal challenges. John Bryson, Barbara Crosby, and Michael Q. Patton (Bryson, Crosby and Patton 2021) talked about leading transformative change at a societal level. Bryson and Crosby (1992) had talked about leadership for the common good already in the beginning of the 1990s. Now they talked about public value creation though the broader lenses of social movements. They likened creating public value to what was going on in a broad social movement to make considerable impact. Kania and Kramer had paved the way earlier by talking about collective impact. Bryson and Crosby took the thought further and essentially tried to scale up the use of the public value framework. Greve and Ysa (2022) collected some of these perspectives in their *Handbook on Strategic Public Management*. In their concluding chapter, they sketched out emerging ideas for strategizing collaborative governance. They presented three challenges: (1) the need to build a holistic model of public governance, (2) how to align the components in strategic public management and (3) achieving agile stability. They then focused on three approaches: (1) co-shaping the future, (2) a mission-oriented approach, and (3) a citizen-centric approach in design thinking and innovation labs. They then sketched out a model, inspired by Bryson and Crosby and their colleagues, on mission-oriented public value creating-systems (focusing on outcomes), strategy management-at-scale (focusing on strategic objectives), and asset and capacity development.

Bryson, Crosby, and Barberg (2022: 109) made their summary conclusions this way: "In closing, we believe it is important to take seriously the need to develop the field of strategic-management-at-scale because so many of the major challenges the world faces require multi-actor, multi-organization, cross-sector responses".

What has happened during the phases described above? In the first phase, the individual public manager is responsible for creating public value. The public managers must be an explorer to use Moore's own characterization who are on the lookout for opportunities to contribute with public value activities. In the second phase, the public manager reaches out to a network of organizations and to citizens in order to get input and to work with them on addressing relevant wicked problems. In the third phase, the ambition is to take it to the next level in the form of strategic management at scale to co-shape the future and address grand challenges. Partnering for public value means being an explorer, reaching out and working together with others, and have ambition of the wider strategic intervention in sight in a systematic way. The model has been gradually expanded over the years. The partnership manager finds him- or herself in a constant dialogue about whom to collaborate with and what new avenues to investigate in a relentless pursuit of public value creation. This could be criticized for being a too technocratic system where the initiative for collaborations are left to the public managers, and where are the politicians by the way? It is not how it functions in reality as politicians and citizens are always the final arbiters of assessing whether any value has been produced. Moore made this very clear in his writings on public value. He also stated that public value creation is an ongoing process. In that way public value creation is a dynamic, not a static system.

Others have called the process for "catalytic governance". Here's what authors of a book of that name learned when they applied the principles:

> Catalytic governance is a process for leading transformative change that engages a wide range of stakeholders in dialogue and empowers then to develop and enact a vision of a desired future. It is a process that is more open, collaborative, forward-looking, and action-oriented than traditional approaches.
>
> (Meredith, Rosell and Davis 2016: 133, the original was in italics)

A companion in a hopeful scenario comes from Torfing et al. (2012) who once wrote after having first a sceptical scenario and a too enthusiastic scenario that:

> In the third and final scenario, we see a cautious expansion of interactive forms of governance based on reflexive and pragmatic choices between different governance modes in relation to particular policy problems and policy tasks. Even a cautious expansion of interactive governance would entail some redefinition of the role and function of the representative and executive institutions of government.
>
> (Torfing et al. 2012: 237)

We have talked in this section about what Sullivan (2022) refers to as the material part of collaboration: how partnerships work and what their mechanisms for working are. Sullivan also frames partnerships in its political context and emphasizes the governments are trying to use partnerships to extend their influence on society. Sullivan furthermore talks about culture and about place, including placed-based partnerships. This section has demonstrated, though, that partnerships are not necessarily tied to a local or regional space, but rather are more national and international given the focus on addressing grand societal challenges.

Partnering for public action give more public managers and more organizations the chance to be onboard when it comes to change processes. More people can have their say and let their voices be heard. Structure conversations and facilitated dialogue can help improving the material that decisions on public value are made on.

The inconclusiveness of public value in partnerships

As the chapters in this book reporting on empirical results testify, the public value coming out of partners remains inconclusive. It is perhaps better to talk about "public value propositions" as Moore (2013) does rather than end results for actions by partnerships. Why is this? First of all, the complexity, or wickedness, of problems indicates almost by definition that quick and visible results are hard to come by. The areas investigated in this book, healthcare, smart cities, climate change, are all characterized by wicked problems to a high degree. Therefore, results in the form of tangible public value for citizens cannot easily be developed. For some, it might be disappointing that we cannot make very firm conclusions that partnerships "work" or "don't work". It all depends, as the old saying goes. Second, many of the empirical investigations have, shall we say, exploratory research designs and many proposes "new avenues for research" rather than display solid empirical results. Quite a number of studies are case studies, either single cases or comparable cases. These provides relevant insight into particular contexts, say in cities in Brazil, or hospitals in Spain, but they hardly form the very solid evidence that are required to make firm conclusions about if partnerships "work" or "don't work". To satisfy audiences who crave solid answers than can be reported in top stories in news media, more research designs with statistical analysis is called for. Third, and as pointed out in Moore's (1995, 2013) framework on creating and recognizing public value, the area is dynamic, meaning that new interventions and responses are going on constantly. As Moore (2013: 409) reminded us:

> it is always part of a continuous learning process in which the public changes its mind about the public values it wants to see produced by and reflected in the actions of government organizations; in which the processes of building legitimacy and support for a given value proposition can be improved and strengthened though better deliberations; and where the mobilization of both external and internal operational capacities becomes both more comprehensive and more intelligently focused on the desired goals.
>
> (Moore 2013: 409–410)

This sentence was written with government organizations in mind, but can just as easily be applied to PPPs.

Democratic concerns

There are some democratic concerns with how partnerships are organized. First of all, they are by nature exclusive in the sense that some are inside the partnership, others are outside the partnership. In a democracy, it is never good to exclude people. A typical concern about partnership is that they send a signal of club government, something that the public is barred from entering. A related issue is here that partnerships are often organized on the basis of a contract between the different partners. The contract is often a private law agreement and will therefore often be confidential and not be open to the public to scrutinize. Also by its very nature, partnerships are set up as a collaboration between different organizations, because the organizations could not solve the problem entirely on their own. Partnerships are therefore bound to cross jurisdictions and organizational boundaries. This would not present a problem if it was a small collaboration on a side-issue that no one cared about. But if partnerships are to become more prevalent across a vast number of public policy areas, then it is not so innocent anymore as Marianna Mazzucato (2013) pointed out in her book on *The Entrepreneurial State* comes close (her subtitle is about debunking the public versus private myth).

Related to democracy is the concept of power. Bryson et al. (2015) has already focused on that power in partnerships is an important feature not to be overlooked. A recent analysis by Gray, Purdy and Ansari (2022) explores the point further from an organization theory perspective. They outline four trajectories that can be present in partnerships in relation to power: (1) collaboration (partners have similar types of power), (2) contention (absence of common purpose and history of conflicts exist), (3) consciousness raising (low-power actors remain on the margins, but their consciousness can be raised), (4) compliance (one or more actors dominate the others). Bannink, Sancino and Sorrentino (2024) goes further and argue that collaborative governance approaches in relation to wicked problems put too much emphasis on consensus and does not, in their view, adequately address the issue of power, and that there are disagreements between actors in a partnership setting.

Some researchers see the fact that contracts are there in writing as a sign of potential improved accountability. The argument is that these agreements would have hidden in policy documents otherwise, but when they are put in a contract, they can, in principle, become more visible. It does require, however, that the contract texts are released and available to the public.

Other researchers have addressed the question directly on accountability in collaboration. (Lee and Ospina 2022) examined the history so far on accountability in collaboration. They came up with a fresh perspective: A process-based approach to accountability in collaboration. They identify three dimensions or stages: (1) the information dimension, (2) the evaluation dimension, and (3) the consequences dimension. In the first dimension, "the actor provides information about his or her conduct to the forum". In the second dimension "the forum evaluates the information and asks for more if insufficient or inappropriate. In the third dimension, "the forum punishes or rewards the actor based on the judgments".

The question is whether partnerships can be rolled back at all? There is not much to suggest that this is happening. If we are to believe the analysis in "the policy state", governments and politicians' appetite for more and new policy will not vanish or vane. Politicians like to make policy and new areas in health and environment comes up all the time, providing politicians with more incentives to demand new policies. And these policies have to be managed and to be put into action which will mainly be done through partnerships as the state's resources may not be enough (if the politicians also want to provide tax reductions at the same time).

So, the debate about the "democratic deficit" of partnerships is old, as is the question of power in partnerships, and is likely to continue for some time, but that does not mean that progress has not been made. Partnerships are better now at opening up, at inviting more stakeholders in, at becoming more transparent, and at communicating better and getting into dialogue with the surrounding society. The closed partnership of yore is not the average partnership anymore. Instead, partnerships are often at the forefront of innovation, of taking new policy initiatives, and governments are also relying more on partnerships.

Partnerships are also becoming prevalent in the international policy area where organizations like the UN, the World Bank, and OECD build many of their activities on partnership ideas and practices.

Practical considerations

Organizations must pay attention to the issues in the policy state that can lead to new partnerships. Because of the dynamics of politics, this is going to be an ongoing task. Pay attention to politics and how it creates new policy. Organizations need to partner up and find organizations to collaborate with on the issues they care about and the kind of public value they want to create. Find out who you want to collaborate with and why. It could be a private firm, an NGO, a government organization – or combination of these. The reason for collaborating may be strategic, but it can also be from a practical point of view of sharing resources and risks. Think of the activity as partnering for public value (in the Mark Moore sense of the term). Organizations must see their organization as an open one that is open to new partnerships. Stay open and allow for memorandum of understandings or partnership agreements. Managers need have the capacities of being bridgebuilders. Managers need to be trained to be partnership managers and to learn of the skills to negotiate and facilitate. The whole of the organization has to be oriented towards more collective leadership. More leaders will be involved in leading the organization. Organizations must see themselves as part of the ecosystem as Tamyko Ysa puts it, or as part of Page and Stone's collaborative architecture. Ecosystems, organizational fields, or whatever you want to call them are necessary for being in this game.

Conclusions

Partnerships are here to stay and become prevalent as part of the policy state. Partnering for public value in Mark Moore's sense is possible. There remain some democratic concerns, but there are also ways to remedy them or address them. The partnership formula (policy state, partnerships, the collaborative self, bridgebuilders, partnering for public value, and the collaborative architecture) provides a framework for understanding partnerships today.

Discussion questions

1 How do partnerships fit into today's world of wicked problems and geopolitical challenges?
2 Why can partnerships said to be producing public value – and for whom?
3 How is the issue of power and democracy handled in the literature on partnerships and what does power mean for managing partnerships?

References

Bannink, Duco; Alessandro Sancino & Maddalena Sorrentino. 2024. "Governance Without We: Wicked Problems and Collaborative Governance" *Public Policy and Administration* 39(3), 301–323.

Bryson, John & Barbara Crosby. 1992. *Leadership for the Common Good. Tackling Public Problems in a Shared-Power World.* San Francisco, CA: Jossey Bass.

Bryson, John; Barbara Crosby; Melissa Stone. 2015. "Designing and Implementing Cross-Sector Collaborations: Needed and Challenging" *Public Administration Review* 75(5), 647–663.

Bryson, John; Barbara Crosby & Michael Q. Patton. 2021. "Leading Social Transformations" *Journal of Change Management* 21(2), 180–202.

Bryson, John; Barbara Crosby & Bill Barberg. 2022. "Public Value Governance and Strategic Public Management" in Greve, Carsten & Ysa, Tamyko. Eds. 2023. *Handbook on Strategic Public Management.* Cheltenham: Edward Elgar, pp. 92–113.

Clarke, Amelia & Andrew Crane. 2018. "Cross-Sector Partnerships for Systemic Change: Systematized Literature Review and Agenda for Further Research" *Journal of Business Ethics* 150, 303–313.

Eggers, William & Donald F. Kettl. 2023. *Bridgebuilders: How Governments Can Transcend Boundaries to Solve Big Problems.* Boston, MA: Harvard Business Review Press.

Gray, Barbara; Jill Purdy & Shahzad Ansari. 2022. "Confronting Power Asymmetries in Partnerships to Address Grand Challenges" *Organization Theory* 3, 1–25.

Greve, Carsten & Tamyko Ysa. Eds. 2022. *Handbook on Strategic Public Management.* Cheltenham: Edward Elgar.

Kettl, Donald F. 2006. "Managing Boundaries in American Government: The Collaborative Imperative" *Public Administration Review* December 2006, special issue, 66, 10–19.

Lee, Seulki & Sonia M. Ospina. 2022. "A Framework for Assessing Accountability in Collaborative Governance: A Process-Based Approach" *Perspectives on Public Management and Governance* 5, 73–75.

Mazzucato, Mariana. 2013. *The Entrepreneurial State. Debunking Public vs. Private Myths.* London: Anthem Press.

Moore, Mark. 1995. *Creating Public Value.* Cambridge, MA: Harvard University Press.

Moore, Mark. 2013. *Recognizing Public Value.* Cambridge, MA: Harvard University Press.

Meredith, Patricia; Steven A. Rosell & Ged R. Davis. 2016. *Catalytic Governance. Leading Change in the Information Age.* Toronto: University of Toronto Press.

Ospina, Sonia; Erica G. Foldy; Gail T. Fairhust & Brad Jackson. 2020. "Collective Dimensions of Leadership: Connecting Theory and Method". *Human Relations* 73(4), 441–463.

Page, Stephen & Melissa M. Stone. 2023: "Collaborative Architecture: Components, Relationships and Implications for Partner Influence" *Perspectives on Public Management and Governance* 6(1), 14–27.

Page, Stephen; John M. Bryson; Melissa M. Stone; Barbara Crosby & Danbi Seo. 2021. "Ambidexterity in Cross-Sector Collaborations Involving Public Organizations" *Public Performance & Management Review*, 44(6), 1161–1190.

Sullivan, Helen. 2022. *Collaboration and Public Policy*. London: Palgrave MacMillan.

Torfing, Jacob; B. Guy Peters; Jon Pierre & Eva Sørensen. 2012. *Interactive Governance*. Oxford: Oxford University Press.

Van Tulder, Rob & Nienke Keen. 2018. "Capturing Collaborative Challenges: Designing Complexity-Sensitive Theories of Change for Cross-Sector Partnerships". *Journal of Business Ethics* 150, 315–322.

Selected readings

Clarke, Amelia & Andrew Crane. 2018. "Cross-Sector Partnerships for Systemic Change: Systematized Literature Review and Agenda for Further Research" *Journal of Business Ethics* 150, 303–313.

This article by Clarke and Crane takes a much-needed look at systemic change in the world of partnerships and present evidence from a review of the literature from a multidisciplinary perspective.

Gray, Barbara; Jill Purdy & Shahzad Asara. 2022. "Confronting Power Asymmetries in Partnerships to Address Grand Challenges" *Organization Theory* 3, 1–25.

A welcome addition to the literature on partnerships that tackles the often-neglected question of power in partnerships head on. These authors enlighten our knowledge on power and how it is always present in partnerships.

Sullivan, Helen. 2022. *Collaboration and Public Policy*. London: Palgrave MacMillan.

A nice tour-de-force on forms and practices and collaborations with many good reflections and an original take on the vast literature on collaboration and partnerships from one of the eminent scholars in the field.

Index